D1125403

GAMES
for the
SOUL

Also by Drew Leder, M.D., Ph.D.
Spiritual Passages: Embracing Life's Sacred Journey

GAMES

for the

SOUL

40 Playful Ways to Find
Fun and Fulfillment
in a Stressful World

Drew Leder, M.D, Ph.D.

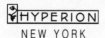

HYPERION

NEW YORK

Library of Congress Cataloging-in-Publication Data

Leder, Drew.
  Games for the soul : 40 playful ways to find fun and fulfillment in a stressful world /
Drew Leder.
    p.   cm.
  Includes bibliographical references.
  ISBN 0-7868-8331-6
  1. Spiritual exercises. 2. Play—Religious aspects. I. Title.
BL624.L45   1998
291.4'46—dc21   98–3798
                                                                                 CIP

Designed by Kay Schuckhart/Blond on Pond

FIRST EDITION

10 9 8 7 6 5 4 3 2 1

For Scott Leder
and
Sarah Leder

Two loved ones who have taught me
how to play.

CONTENTS

Introduction: Why This Book and How to Use It xi

Part One: CELEBRATING THE ORDINARY 1
1. Dayeinu! 4
2. The Use of the Useless 8
3. My Award-Winning Day 13
4. Surfing the Psalm 18
5. Thinking to Thank 23

Part Two: ACCEPTANCE and FORGIVENESS 29
6. Blessed Imperfection 32
7. Life's Perfect Lessons 37
8. Children's World 42
9. Unpointing the Finger 47
10. The Favorable Judge 51

Part Three: LOVING THE SELF 57
11. The Child Within 60
12. Kissing the Boo-Boo 65
13. The Affirmative No 69
14. Seeing Your Shadow 75
15. Home Sweet Home 81

Part **F**our: **T**HE **G**ENEROUS **H**EART 87

16. WLUV 90
17. God in Disguise 96
18. Give, Give, Give 100
19. LEGGO and Let God 104
20. Golden-Ruling 110

Part **F**ive: **C**ONTACTING THE **D**IVINE 115

21. The (Not So) Imaginary Friend 118
22. The Inner Elder 123
23. Plugging In 128
24. Lectio Divina 133
25. God Letters 139

Part **S**ix: **C**LAIMING **I**NNER **F**REEDOM 145

26. The Witness Protection Program 148
27. Breathing ABCs 153
28. About Face! 158
29. A Word to the Wise 163
30. Unselfing Yourself 167

Part **S**even: **T**HE **W**ONDER *o**f* **C**REATION 173

31. Entering the Mind of Nature 176
32. Outside In 180
33. Coming to Our Senses 185
34. The Artist's Eye 190
35. Listening to Your Body 194

Part Eight: DANCING with TIME and ETERNITY 201

36.   The Take-Your-Time Tango 204
37.   Present! 209
38.   Time Traveling 213
39.   Your Last, Best Day 219
40.   The Eternal Day 223

Epilogue: Where Do I Go from Here? 227
Acknowledgments 232

INTRODUCTION

WHY THIS BOOK
and HOW TO USE IT

Who says spiritual growth can't be fun? I certainly did for a long time. I was as grim as they come.

My family history included cancer and suicide, each of which left its mark. A hard worker by training, I tried to work things out using therapy and spiritual tools.

I joined a Twelve Step program to treat a variety of compulsive problems. This program has saved my life. But all too often (due to that compulsive bent), I used it as a weapon to turn against myself. "I must be more unselfish. I must be more prayerful. I must admit my wrongdoings, and in the future work harder."

A certain notion of spirituality underlay these struggles. Didn't the world's sacred traditions agree (I thought) that the path to the divine was arduous? That it involved discipline, sacrifice, and renunciation? Nothing to do but roll up my sleeves and set to work clearing boulders. This I did, but with a certain reluctance. Secretly I longed to have fun.

Then a funny thing happened on my spiritual journey. I discovered that it could be fun. Or, to put it more strongly, that it had to be fun for me to wish to go forward. I felt a Power reach out to me in playful ways. "Lighten up," He/She/It seemed to say. "I am your friend and playmate, not some harsh taskmaster. I want to teach you how to dance through life, not stagger beneath your burdens."

"The reason angels can fly is that they take themselves so lightly," wrote G. K. Chesterton. Only by lightening up, I sensed, could I spread some light to others.

Around this time a teacher entered my life, small but potent. Her name is Sarah. She's my now two-year-old daughter. She can light up a room at a hundred paces with megawatts of play-energy. Play is how she relates to the world. It is her tool of concentration, learning, and growth, her instrument of delight. Hey, if it's good enough for a two-year-old, why not her forty-two-year-old dad? "Be like a little child," says Matthew 18:3 in the New Testament, "or you cannot enter the kingdom of Heaven."

I found myself embarking on something new, something I call "the way of play." This new path did not lead me to abandon the Twelve Step program. Its spiritual disciplines remain central and necessary to my life. But I found I could make better use of such disciplines the more I envisioned them as games. For games they were when I looked beneath the surface. It seems a weighty matter to "practice the presence of God" by prayer throughout the day. But isn't this like the child who chatters away to an unseen friend? That's play, not work. It's a pleasure to share life's ups and downs with an ever-present companion.

Or, to take a different example, it can seem like hard work to reform the mind by cultivating positive thoughts. (Imagine furrowing your brow as you tackle the task.) But real progress began when I made it into a game. Could I think of ten positive things I did, others did, and Spirit did in my life that very day? (So what if it's small—add it to the list.) And why not have an awards ceremony for the outstanding one in each category?

I began to think of all spiritual disciplines as games—perhaps the most challenging and meaningful of games—but games nonetheless. And I realized that the way of play was a part of all religions. St. Paul proclaimed himself a "fool for Christ." Jews honor the Sabbath, that time to stop working and to take pleasure in life. Hindus say that the universe was created as *lila*, divine play. (After all, the Omnipresent Eternal One needed something to do.) Muslim Sufis teach through jokes about Mulla Nasrudin, a laughable sage/fool. Native Americans celebrate bawdy trickster-figures. (Try attending a Cherokee "Booger Event.") Buddhists practice meditative games of breathing, attention, and joyful presence. Zen teachers poke fun at dogma, as in master Feng's pronouncement: "The Buddha is a bullheaded jail keeper, and the Patriarchs are horse-faced old maids!" It seemed the whole world was playing with Spirit in a thousand delightful ways.

This book is an invitation for you to play, too. Drawing on the world's sacred traditions, it presents forty different games for the soul. They are designed to help you grow in wisdom, love, and spirituality. And, oh yeah, to have this growth be fun.

How can you best utilize this book? Pretend you've been invited to a grand feast. Set before you is an array of dishes, these forty games. You may wish at some point to take a taste of every one. Some of them may not suit your palate. But those you find most to your liking you can order as main courses. That is, you can play those games for a long while, or even the rest of your life.

As at a buffet, feel free to move about, sampling dishes in the order you please. True, the book is structured in a linear way: Each section of games clusters around a single theme, which in turn leads to the focus of the next section. For example, games of "Loving the Self" in Part Three help prepare us to outflow love to others, as in games of "The Generous Heart" in Part Four. Still, it can work in the reverse. Giving to others helps us develop self-love. And both kinds of love can be unleashed by "Contacting the Divine," the theme of Part Five. So where to begin and what order to go in? It's up to you. At times, you might even turn it over to the universe by opening the book at random.

And how long should you stay with any given game? Again, it's your decision. Sampled as an appetizer, each game is designed to be played in one day. In fact, no game demands more than about twenty minutes of your time. However, as with most things in life, the more you put in, the more rewards you get back. So consider playing each game with intensity, returning to it throughout the day or extending it for a longer period. I found three days optimal for learning a game: one to give it a test-run; the second to make adjustments; the third to help it settle into a habit.

To turn that game into a main course, simply stay with it indefinitely, or build it into your life schedule. For example, you might make Monday (just for a challenge) your day for "Thinking to Thank"; Tuesday, your day to write a "God Letter"; and so on through the week.

As you progress through the book, you can also mix and match games in synergistic combinations. Say you're playing at being "Present!" to the moment, but your crazy schedule pulls you away. Match it with "The Take-Your-Time Tango," a game designed to help you slow down.

As important as which games you play, and when, is *how* you choose to play them. For each game, I provide detailed suggestions. After all, games need structure and rules. I also supply helpful hints based on my own experience. Still, people are very different in their style of play. Part of the fun is discovering your own.

You may enjoy meeting challenges and striving for personal bests. If so, you can set up goals for each game. How many things can you be thankful for? Can you remember Spirit at least once every hour? Can you find a way to judge more favorably that person whom you *most* dislike?

On the other hand, such goal-setting may feel too pressured for you. Fixed goals can take away fun and spontaneity and, if not met, be a trigger for self-attack. If so, avoid them like the plague. Structure each game in a way that seems comfortable, free from notions of success and failure. And remember to be patient with yourself. Some of these games go against the habits of a lifetime. Don't expect to be transformed into a loving, generous, grateful saint by tomorrow noon at the latest.

Let me, however, offer a few suggestions that might help your play bear fruit. First, consider starting a game-journal. This is a place to chart positive results and explore blocks that arise. You can write lists, draw pictures, compose poems, and free-associate based on each game as you play. Of course, you don't have to write a blessed thing. (Though a college professor, I won't be collecting your journals.) But you may find that writing helps you to solidify and absorb the benefits of each game.

Another tactic you may find useful is something I call the game-mantra. Make up a brief phrase that reinforces the theme of the game you're about to play. For a game on accepting imperfection, you could use a reminder like "To err is human"; an affirmation such as "I'm *enough* just as I am"; or a prayer like "Lord, fill my heart with forgiveness." Let this mantra be your friend. When you remember, repeat it in your mind throughout the day (see #23, "Plugging In"). It's likely to strengthen your play. Also watch out for mental demons that will counterattack the games. "This is stupid." "I've no time." "I'm doing it wrong." Thank these thoughts for sharing, then tell them to go take a hike. They can't get you if you don't let them.

Then, too, remember you're not alone. You have access to a divine Gamemaster, whether you conceive of this as God, Allah, Buddha-Nature, the Goddess, Christ, the Tao, or your own higher Self. You may feel intuitively led to certain games at certain times, or to strategies for how best to play. Listen to this inner guidance. "The spirit blows where it will . . . you do not know where it comes from, or where it goes" (John 3:8). Yes, but following its lead can be the greatest game of all.

Along with divine guidance, you might also draw on divine *power*. Early in my own Twelve Step work I realized that I wasn't going to get far under my own steam. I simply had too obsessive a mind that wouldn't obey my directions. So self-help books didn't work for me. I needed to convert them into spiritual-help books by relying on a Power greater than myself. Only then could I practice those excellent principles that self-help books contain.

Divine aid is a great thing, but so is that which we receive from other people. Consider finding one or more partners with whom to play these games. Of course, there's nothing wrong with using this book on your own. Some of my best childhood games I played alone, with myself as pitcher, batter, and everyone else (yet somehow my team always won). Still, a playmate can add fun and value. You may find yourself taking the games more seriously (or playfully), when there's another to whom you're accountable, and with whom you can nonjudgmentally discuss problems and successes. So why not ask a good friend to play along, or even a family member? (The games work well for preteens to great-grandparents.) The family that plays together stays together, especially when the play triggers meaningful talk. The book is also suitable for group use, through a place of worship, service organization, educational setting, or wherever else strikes your fancy.

In addition to your peers, you also have access to great teachers, past and present, and from around the world. They're in any bookstore or library just waiting to be consulted. So don't hesitate to use their help. At the end of each game, I supply a short list of related readings. These are books that address the game's theme and methods in far more detail than I possibly could. If you want to convert a game from appetizer to main dish—an ongoing practice in your life—consider looking up these works. Their guidance and inspiration may prove invaluable. Their authors may also direct you to other works, and so on. You can go as far as you wish.

And where, in the long run, do you want to go? That's the subject of the book's last chapter. I give suggestions for how to turn the way of play into a way of life. Finally, you may range beyond these games to ones you invent yourself.

So I hope you enjoy the journey you're commencing. It's the light-hearted path to enlightenment.

Part One

Celebrating

the Ordinary

it's always best to begin at the beginning. And where is that? Right here, right now, as you read this book in the midst of your everyday life. Sometimes the spiritual quest is understood as that which transports us elsewhere—to peak experiences, divine visitations, otherworldly realms. Such can happen. But teachers across the world agree: The sacred is here among us, and within. If you can't find it in your own backyard you will search the world over in vain. In *The Sayings of the Lay Disciple Ho*, Zen poet P'ang-yun described enlightenment:

> *My daily activities are no different,*
> *Only I'm in harmony with them . . .*
> *Drawing water, chopping wood,*
> *How marvelous, what a miracle!*

It's in drawing water, chopping wood—or more likely nowadays, in taking out the garbage, shopping at the supermarket, doing our job, playing with our children—that we can best find the wholeness we seek. But this is easier said than done. So often our days are fragmented as we lurch from one demand to the next. Ordinary duties do not seem marvelous and miraculous; they're but items to be crossed off a to-do list which quickly spawns more items.

The games in this section are designed to help us live anew. They focus on a shift of attitude. Through becoming more grateful, more peaceful, more celebratory, we realize the gifts that surround us. In *The Way of Man According to the Teaching of Hasidism,* Martin Buber describes the goal in a Jewish idiom:

> *It is said of a certain Talmudic master that the paths of heaven were as bright to him as the streets of his native town. Hasidism inverts the order: It is a greater thing if the streets of a man's native town are as bright to him as the paths of heaven. For it is here, where we stand, that we should try to make shine the light of the hidden divine life.*

These are games to aid that process. If God is playing hide-and-seek in the world, they can help us to call out, "Found you!"

1. DAYEINU!

*Had God fed us with manna and not given us
the Sabbath, Dayeinu!
Had God given us the Sabbath and not brought
us to Mount Sinai, Dayeinu!
Had God brought us to Mount Sinai and not
given us the Torah, Dayeinu!
Had God given us the Torah and not led us into
the land of Israel, Dayeinu!*

—*A Passover Haggadah*, ed. Herbert Bronstein

n the Passover seder, Jews commemorate the miracle of the exodus from Egypt. Recalling each element of what God did for the Israelites, a celebrant cries out, "Dayeinu!" (pronounced die-ay-noo) which literally means "enough," or "it would have been enough." It would have been enough, by itself, to receive manna in the desert; or the grace of the Sabbath; or the sacred books of the Torah—the list goes on and on. Any of these blessings, on its own, would have been fulfilling, and yet Spirit heaped them one atop another in a marvelous profligacy of riches.

As you go through the day, proclaim to yourself time and again in thought (or aloud if no one's around to think you crazy), "Dayeinu!" At a joyful event—a nice breakfast, perhaps—use this to awaken to the fullness of the moment. "A heap of pancakes, maple syrup, my family's gathered and actually getting along—this is enough." At more difficult times, use "Dayeinu!" as a challenge to see them afresh. Perhaps you're cleaning up the mess after that breakfast when you remember to repeat to yourself "Dayeinu!" Dayeinu? Yes, this, too, is enough: the calming of chaos back into order while wiping the counters clean. In this way, use "Dayeinu!" as a repetitive mantra to call yourself back to wholeness.

Then, too, before retiring at night, take a few minutes to recollect the day and celebrate the many blessings you received. For example, you might say (in mental, spoken, or written form): "Had I only spent that time reading my daughter fairy-tales, Dayeinu! Had I only gone for that walk with the sun and wind in my face, Dayeinu!" Recite the litany of sacred blessings the day has laid at your doorstep.

See how many dayeinus you can uncover. Perhaps it's easy to find two or three. But what if each day, you search out at least five or ten (or some such goal)? A slew of small treasures may come to light that a cursory scan would miss.

You might also focus on particular areas of your life. Perhaps you enjoy spending time with the kids, but find your nine-to-five world frustrating. Can you locate dayeinus even at work? Or maybe your issue is the opposite—hanging on to dayeinus when stuck in the house on a rainy day with a two-year-old. For even small successes, give yourself a pat on the back and a "Dayeinu!" to the grace-filled universe.

Helpful Hints

Fake it till you make it. You may feel you're not having much of a Dayeinu-day. The dog peed on the living room carpet, an unexpected bill arrived in the mail, and everything blew up at work. So what? Fake it till you make it. That is, instead of abandoning the game, redouble your efforts to find dayeinus even if it feels artificial. This discipline of mind, with time, can infiltrate your heart. You slowly begin to experience what at first seemed but pretense.

Use ritual. The evening Dayeinu-recitation can become even more powerful if, like the Passover seder, you surround it with sacred ceremony. You might choose a special place and time— light candles, use a meditation cushion—whatever works for you. Or keep it simple. Dayeinus while brushing your teeth at night, or while drifting off to sleep, can themselves become soothing rituals.

Related Readings

Herbert Bronstein, ed. *A Passover Haggadah.* New York: Central Conference of American Rabbis, 1974. This, or any number of other guides to the Passover ritual, can help clarify the Dayeinu consciousness at the heart of Judaism.

Frederic and Mary Ann Brussat. *Spiritual Literacy: Reading the Sacred in Everyday Life.* New York: Scribner, 1996. A rich collection of excerpts from contemporary spiritual writers, organized into helpful categories such as "nature," "leisure," and "relationships."

Stewart W. Holmes and Chimyo Horioka. *Zen Art for Meditation.* Rutland, VT: Charles E. Tuttle, 1973. Zen Buddhism says that *samsara* (the everyday world) is itself *nirvana* (bliss, transcendence) if we but embrace the moment fully.

7

2. THE USE *of the* USELESS

Do you want to work upon the world and improve it?
It won't work.

The world is sacred.
It can't be improved.
If you try to fix it, you'll ruin it.
If you try to grasp it, you'll lose it.

—Lao Tzu, *Tao te Ching*

f there's one thing the modern world teaches us it's to be cease-lessly productive. "Time is money" as long as it's profitably spent. The upshot: We rush through life trying to do, do, do, measuring our self-worth by our usefulness.

But we pay a price for this lifestyle. With all the focus on doing, we lose the ability to simply be still, centered in the moment. Ever working, we lose access to the child's joy in "useless" play. Bent on improving the world, we ruin its ecology. Our inner ecology also suffers, as our compulsion to do obliterates the spiritual life. Who has "useless" time anymore for retreats, for contemplation, for waiting on that still, small voice within?

Today, rediscover the profound use of the useless. Commit to doing three or more useless things—at least one in the morning, one in the afternoon, and one in the evening. How so, if the usual busy day looms? These useless activities need not require large chunks of time. What's important is that they allow you (force you?) to jump off the productivity treadmill and rediscover the joy of life.

How best to be useless? Let your heart be your guide. Perhaps you choose an early walk as your morning useless-time. A breeze sways the trees as you wander still streets. Why? No purpose. Leaves whisper; you walk; that's all. Later, at the office, you need something to relieve the mounting pressure of afternoon deadlines. In your briefcase, amidst all the important papers, you've slipped a favorite book of verse. Each hour, on the hour, you pull it out and read one poem, savoring it like a cool drink. How delightfully useless! If you're afraid you'll get caught, sneak your poem in the bathroom.

The evening? Now there's an especially good time to be useless. Sure, there's dinner to be made, kids to be washed and bedded, bills to be paid (come to think of it, the office wasn't half-bad). But friends and families need useless time: They grow on it like corn in the night. Let's order out for pizza; consume it on the back porch; play a silly game of charades. We'll be useful tomorrow.

In addition to your three useless activities, try to bring a "useless" attitude to other things you do during the day. When being "useful" we view tasks primarily as means to an end. We finish projects, earn paychecks, accomplish chores, win praise, and cross off items from our list. We're focused on attaining a desired product.

Today, attend more to the *process* than the product. Don't shower to get clean. Just explore the feeling of warm-water-needles tickling your flesh. How interesting. Don't cook to get that damn dinner on the table. Just toss the salad and stir the noodles like a kitchen-dance enjoyed for itself. The chores will still get done. But all the while (don't tell anyone) you're being useless.

And instead of making a list of useful things to get done, why not reverse matters? Keep a list of *useless* things to do or be. Note the three special activities you chose, and the other tasks you render useless through focusing on process, not product. The object of this list is not to cross items off, but to add them on. What better way to add joy to your life?

Helpful Hints

Cultivate useless places. We often associate different places with definite activities and mindsets. You might find it hard to be useless when perched at your cluttered office desk. In that case, leave. Take a lunchtime stroll in a nearby park. Or maybe you feel assaulted by a thousand things to do as soon as you walk in your house. If so, you might find an alcove you could turn into a special space. Put up a curtain. Reserve this room exclusively for "useless" activities like prayer, reading, and meditation. Whenever you enter, your mind will breathe a pleasant sigh of relief.

It's hard to be easy. You may find that easing up from your productive focus proves a hard thing indeed. "Getting things done" earns approval and provides a sense of accomplishment. Feeling useless may trigger fear or guilt.

If it helps, remind yourself that being useless is today's assignment. You *have* to do it. It will help you return to your day's work refreshed. It will also be *useful* for your spiritual progress. Feeling better already? With time, you may be able to let go of this crutch and be useless more uselessly.

Related Readings

Abraham Joshua Heschel. *The Sabbath*. New York: Farrar, Straus and Giroux, 1951. An eloquent meditation on the Jewish ritual of the Sabbath, wherein all work ceases and inner peace is reclaimed.

Sue Monk Kidd. *When the Heart Waits: Spiritual Direction for Life's Sacred Questions*. San Francisco: HarperSanFrancisco, 1990. The author explores the role of stillness and waiting as part of the spiritual quest. (Also see the splendid writings of the Trappist monk, Thomas Merton, concerning the monastic life.)

Lao-tzu, version by Stephen Mitchell. *Tao te Ching*. New York: HarperPerennial, 1988. This Taoist classic, of which there are many good translations, discusses the useful uselessness of the enlightened sage. (See, as well, the Taoist works of Chuang Tzu.)

3. My Award-Winning Day

What you think about grows. Whatever you allow to occupy your mind you magnify in your own life. Whether the subject of your thought be good or bad, the law works and the condition grows. . . . The more you think about your grievances or the injustices that you have suffered, the more such trials will you continue to receive; and the more you think of the good fortune you have had, the more good fortune will come to you.

—Emmet Fox, *Make Your Life Worthwhile*

he Academy Awards and other such ceremonies are enormously popular. They celebrate outstanding accomplishments in a variety of endeavors. It's not only the public, but the industry that likes them. They focus attention on the nominees and effectively sell their products.

Why not turn this device toward spiritual ends? In this game, focus attention on the good in and around you by presenting daily awards. The product you're selling is nothing less than a fulfilling experience of life.

You might work initially with three categories. The first is My Positive Accomplishments. As you go through the day, note things you have done well: unselfish acts, constructive approaches to problems, moments of kindness to yourself and others. Perhaps you were courteous to a next-door neighbor, or tackled a chore you'd been putting off. Add it to the list you're keeping mentally or on paper.

The second category is Positive Accomplishments of Others. Keep track of the good things that those around you do this day. Your child-care provider greets your kid with a hug; she treats him like one of her own. Today, don't just take that for granted. Put it on the list. After arriving on the job, a co-worker offers to bring you coffee. That's considerate. On the list it goes.

The third category is something like Special Graces from God or the Universe. Here note any positives that Spirit has sent your way: a parking space appearing when you desperately needed one; some relief from fear as a result of prayer; a well-timed phone call from an old friend; coming home at night to a basically happy marriage. Search out blessings you might otherwise overlook.

All day you've been assembling your nominees. In the evening hold an awards ceremony, selecting an outstanding winner from each category. Consider the candidates carefully before making your choice. "The winner of My Most Positive Accomplishment is . . . (drumroll please) . . . Not yelling at the kids even when they were driving me crazy! For me, that's a big accomplishment." Sure, there are no spotlights and swelling theme music, no photographers and glitz. Nonetheless, graciously accept your Oscar. ("I'd like to thank my friend, Mary, who helped make this possible by listening to me complain.") Then go on to the other categories, and present awards to another person, and then to God or the helpful Universe, specifying in each case what it is for, and mentally congratulating winners and worthy runners-up.

You may find this is a hard game to keep in your head. Throughout the day, or at night, you might make a three-column list of nominees. It can help to set a goal for the number in each category, such as five, or seven, or even ten. At day's end, you might circle the winners, or draw in a little Oscar statuette.

Facing a difficult choice, you may feel hesitant to award just one winner in a category. Perhaps the day's mail brought an unexpected gift from your parents. Then, too, when you arrived home dog-tired and grumpy, your partner was kind beyond the call of duty. You don't want to rank one against the other. Simply invent new categories, like the Generosity Award, or the Award for Putting Up with My Stuff. In that area, someday your partner might even merit a (coveted) Lifetime Achievement Award.

Helpful Hints

Think small. You may feel that some of the day's accomplishments and gifts are simply too small to matter. "So I handled that project at work competently. I'm supposed to. That's my job. So it was a fresh, spring day, not too cool or hot. That's just what you expect in May." Count these anyway, at least as nominees, if not grand-prize winners. This game is designed to heighten your awareness of precisely what you've taken for granted.

Try to keep your lists even. You may find that one list is lengthening as another lags behind. Perhaps it's easier to see the goodness in others than in yourself, or vice-versa. Or maybe it's a strain to recognize the graces of God/the Universe—your mind just doesn't work that way. So at midday you have eight items on one list, but only three on another. Try to find more nominees for the latter to even things up. That will encourage you to go forward in whatever area you find a challenge.

Use this game when off-course. During the day there may be times when negative thoughts throw you out of kilter: "I can't believe I left my briefcase at home like an idiot." This is a good

16

time to counteract such thoughts by noting positive things you've done. Or else you feel, "Nothing, but nothing is going right." It's a good time to look for the day's hidden graces. In this way, use this game like a compass and rudder to correct your course as needed.

Related Readings

David D. Burns. *Feeling Good: The New Mood Therapy.* New York: Avon Books, 1980. A physician's practical introduction to "cognitive therapy": a way to relieve depression and anxiety through the conscious management of thought.

Emmet Fox. *Make Your Life Worthwhile.* San Francisco: HarperSanFrancisco, 1946. In this and other books, Fox discusses how positive thinking can improve our inner and outer lives and help us to spiritually advance.

4. SURFING the ☀ PSALM

The Lord is my Shepherd. I shall not want.
(S)He maketh me to lie down in green pastures.
(S)He leadeth me beside the still waters.
(S)He restoreth my soul.
(S)He leadeth me in the paths of righteousness for his (her) name's sake.
Yea, though I walk through the valley of the shadow of death, I will fear
no evil for thou art with me.
Thy rod and thy staff they comfort me.
Thou preparest a table before me in the presence of mine enemies.
Thou anointest my head with oil.
My cup runneth over.
Surely goodness and mercy shall follow me all the days of my life
And I will dwell in the house of the Lord forever.
—Psalm 23

❧

Composed over two thousand years ago, let this sacred song guide your path today. Begin by reading it over with care in the morning. Then, throughout the day, use individual lines as a prayer or "mantra" you repeat inside your mind. (See #23, "Plugging In" for more detail on mantra-techniques.)

Above, I've divided the psalm into twelve lines. Each expresses a self-contained positive thought and image. In a linear version of the game, begin at the beginning and work through the psalm at the rate of about a line an hour. Say you crawl out of bed at 7:00 A.M. For that first hour say again and again in your mind, "The Lord is my shepherd. I shall not want." Taking your morning shower, you're already laying claim to the guidance of a loving Spirit.

Around 8:00 A.M. (a watch-alarm that beeps the hour helps) go on to the next line: "(S)He maketh me to lie down in green pastures." Huh? You're currently stuck in traffic, frustration building inside. Still, using this line can help you rethink the situation. Maybe even the crowded expressway can be your "green pasture." Relax. Breathe deeply. "Lie down" mentally in calm. You're not just stuck in traffic—you're resting.

In such a way, let the psalm turn your day into a journey guided by Spirit. You will find still-points, trudge down paths, and negotiate dark valleys. Despite the challenges, you will emerge to dine with God, and bed down safely in your spiritual home.

At about a line an hour, you may be surprised at how the structure of the day seems to match that of the psalm. But be flexible. Your progress through this prayer can slow or speed up to match the rhythm of events.

Or get more radical still. We're used to channel-surfing for a good TV show, or surfing the Internet for information. Why not do the same with a sacred text, in search of inspiration? In a second version of the game, simply surf the psalm for whatever line best meets the needs of the moment. Perhaps a work deadline throws you into a tizzy. You grab onto the phrase: "(S)He leadeth me beside the still waters." The words, repeated within, help you to calm and center. That is, until your computer crashes. Time for a new line: "Yea, though I walk through the valley of the shadow of death, I will fear no evil." The dark screen looks like death, but let's get real: Not that much work was lost. These things happen. No need to panic . . . I will fear no evil.

Later, the computer up and running, you complete the job, meet the deadline, and get the boss off your back. Time, perhaps, to use "My cup runneth over!" It's a reminder to celebrate life's blessings.

Over time, the psalm can even yield insights into the general pattern and needs of your life. What tends to be your valley of the shadow of death—times of anxious stress, flare-ups of a chronic ailment, or periodic depression? And what are the green pastures, and still waters, that restore your soul? You might take a little time to meditate deeply on each line. Seek answers. Write them down. Free associate. This psalm can be a lifeline to the divine.

Helpful Hints

Alter the words as needed. When turning a line from the psalm into a repeated mantra, feel free to alter the wording. "Surely goodness and mercy shall follow me all the days of my life" may seem a bit cumbersome. If so, condense it to "goodness and mercy are with me," or "I'm surrounded by love." What matters is the fundamental idea. Express it as you wish.

Affirm the good. It may seem that what you are asserting ("He restoreth my soul") at times directly contradicts reality ("I'm falling apart!"). Never mind. Repeat the words anyway with as much zeal as you can muster. By affirming what you wish for, you help it begin to manifest.

Get sensual. Don't just think the words of the psalm, but sink into its sensual images. What is the table like that God prepares, even in the presence of your enemies? Is the anointing oil on your forehead cool or warm? How's your room in the house of the Lord furnished? These vivid images will reach not only into your mind, but your body, emotions, and spirit.

Choose your own. The technique used with Psalm 23 is equally applicable to other sacred passages. The psalms themselves pro-

21

vide an abundance of riches. See, for example, portions of Psalms 27, 46, 91, or a multitude of others. Or choose any favorite prayer or passage (see #24 "Lectio Divina") and work with it line-by-line. There's an ocean of spiritual writings out there, so pick your wave and surf on!

Related Readings

Eknath Easwaran, ed. *God Makes the Rivers to Flow: Selections from the Sacred Literature of the World Chosen for Daily Meditation.* Petaluma, CA: Nilgiri Press, 1982. A beautiful collection of passages drawn from a variety of spiritual traditions.

Philip Keller. *A Shepherd Looks at Psalm 23.* New York: Zondervan, 1970. Written from a Christian perspective, this book presents a vivid analysis of the psalm drawing on the experience of a modern-day sheepowner and rancher.

Stephen Mitchell. *A Book of Psalms.* New York: HarperCollins, 1993. This and other contemporary translations can help reawaken us to the powerful imagery of the psalms. (But in some ways the King James version is still unbeatable.)

5. THINKING to THANK

What counts on your path to fulfillment is that we remember the great truth that moments of surprise want to teach us: Everything is gratuitous, everything is gift. The degree to which we are awake to this truth is the measure of our gratefulness. And gratefulness is the measure of our aliveness. Are we not dead to whatever we take for granted?

—Brother David Steindl-Rast, *Gratefulness, the Heart of Prayer*

a s you go through the day, see how many things you can offer thanks for: a tingling hot shower; the smell of coffee percolating; your general good health (not counting that trick knee); a job that pays the bills; a good laugh with co-workers. . . . You get the idea. Cultivate an attitude of gratitude.

To make this exercise more vivid, turn that gratitude into specific acts of thanksgiving. Mentally, say "Thank you, God" or "Thank you, world" each time you notice a blessing. "Thanks God, for giving me a family that loves me (even if that love sometimes takes strange forms). As for my splitting headache, thanks for aspirin." This may feel a bit sappy and artificial. Yet with practice, the artifice turns into habit, engendering a grateful heart.

To stimulate this awareness during the day, instead of coffee-breaks you might take little thank-you breaks. You can use devices that help to stimulate ideas. For example, divide your life into categories (work; family; nature; health and safety; special pleasures) and see if you can find things to be thankful for in each and every area. Or use the alphabet as a thought-provoker. Find something to be grateful for that starts with **A** (your *animals* perhaps, a cat and a hamster), then **B** (your favorite *books*), and on down the line. Some letters will be harder than others, but see how many you can fill in.

Also thank the people around you for any kind or helpful acts. They may be surprised, and you may feel embarrassed by these unusual shows of gratitude. Your kids are used to having their surly moods critiqued. But say instead, "Thanks for your cheerfulness this morning—it makes the day a little brighter," and their initial response will be "Huh?"

Still, gratitude engenders good feelings in both the giver and receiver. You may even find people thanking you for thinking to thank them.

Helpful Hints

Consider thank-you cards. Did your mother ever nudge you to "be sure to write a thank-you card"? It's a chore when done out of duty, but a joy when the sentiment is real. You might buy a packet of thank-you cards in preparation for this game. Practice gratitude by popping one in the mail (or leaving it on an appropriate desk, pillow, or kitchen table) to recognize another's kind acts. Then, too, you might write a thank-you card to God for special (or ordinary) blessings received. An added bonus: Since Spirit is omnipresent and omniscient you don't even have to spend on postage.

25

Find the light coming through the crack. It's unlikely your life is seamlessly smooth. In fact, it's probably riddled with a number of cracks: difficulties, disappointments, trying people and circumstances. Instead of just wishing them away, imagine that each crack allows some light to shine through. That is, see the blessings hidden amidst the hardships. Perhaps you're struggling with an unhappy relationship. Are there ways this is forcing you to grow? Or maybe you're sidelined with an injury. Perhaps this is an opportunity to rest and do some inner work. In such ways, try to find the light coming through the crack, and offer thanks even for your problems.

Recognize your resistance. Thinking to thank sounds like a fun and easy game until you run head-first into blocks. Subconscious guilt may make you feel undeserving of blessings. Or you might have a hard time imagining a Higher Power who loves you enough to shower you with gifts. Perhaps you're the independent sort, uncomfortable with acknowledging reliance on those around you. Then, too, others have things that you don't; you may lapse into jealousy and self-pity. Or perhaps you're used to focusing on future goals rather than present gifts.

If such problems arise, don't feel like a failure. Simply note them nonjudgmentally. This game, and some of the others—on being present, cultivating self-love, and contacting the divine— may help you meet these challenges.

Related Readings

Patricia Gits Opatz. *The Pleasure of God's Company.* Collegeville, MN: The Liturgical Press, 1985. Brief essays on enjoying God and life; see especially "Thanks for Everything."

Brother David Steindl-Rast. *Gratefulness, the Heart of Prayer.* New York: Paulist Press, 1984. This Benedictine monk explores the notion that all prayer is essentially an act of gratitude.

27

Part Two
ACCEPTANCE and
FORGIVENESS

the preceding games were about celebrating the ordinary. However, as soon as we set out to do so, we may encounter an obstacle on our path about as subtle as a boulder. It's not just that the ordinary is so . . . well . . . ordinary. With practice we can search out its blessings. The problem is that the ordinary is also so filled with curses, afflictions, and minor annoyances that we sometimes want to scream. A stray dog overturns the garbage. The checkbook won't stay balanced. A co-worker's personality is vaguely reminiscent of fingernails screeching on a blackboard. And a partner's bathroom habits—don't get me started! The list of grievances can go on and on. It might be easier to celebrate the ordinary, it seems, if only the ordinary were different.

But it's not. That's the catch. Somehow we must find joy in a universe that defies our wishes and demands. Of course, we should do what we can, personally and through social activism, to forge a better world. But we also have to accept life on life's terms. Imperfection reigns. Both we and our neighbors are prone to error. Frustrations, disappointments, and failures seem to be part of life's curriculum. The world is a sad, joyful, screwed-up place.

What to do? A Hindu master, Ramana Maharshi, said, "Wanting to reform the world without discovering one's true self is like trying to cover the world with leather to avoid the pain of walking on stones and thorns. It is much simpler to wear shoes." Yes, but too often we choose the former tactic: We seek to criticize, control, and change things around us. Sometimes it seems we'll need enough leather to cover the known universe. (If we find life-forms on other planets, they'll probably be annoying, too.) Plus, others have their own redecorating plans which interfere with ours.

The games in this section are about choosing instead to put on shoes. That is, to change our own point of view; accept reality; let go of demands; learn from our difficulties; and forgive both self and others. As we don these shoes, a surprising thing occurs. We can walk down even the rough streets of life with a little more ease and comfort.

6. BLESSED
IMPERFECTION

Spirituality begins with the acceptance that our fractured being, our imperfection, simply is: There is no one to "blame" for our errors—neither ourselves nor anyone nor anything else. Spirituality helps us first to see, and then to understand, and eventually to accept the imperfection that lies at the very core of our human be-ing. Spirituality accepts that "If a thing is worth doing it is worth doing badly."

—Ernest Kurtz and Katherine Ketcham, *The Spirituality of Imperfection*

how often we launch our day like a newly christened cruise ship, hoping for the best. And how often the ship founders and sinks. Why? We've hit an iceberg of frustration. We're upset with some mistake we've made, or the faults of others. On the surface, it's no big deal. But the bulk of the iceberg lies buried beneath. Subconscious resentments, despair, and guilt build up as we focus on such failings.

How to avoid those icebergs before they are upon us? We have to learn to let go, and let go, and let go again, to maintain the open seas.

Let go of what? Our own mistakes; the errors of others; the imperfection that surrounds us.

Today, whenever you see a mistake being made, let it go as quickly as you can. Don't linger in self-righteous judgment. Don't demand that the miscreants (whether yourself or others) by-God pay for their sins. Just let it go at once and sail free.

Perhaps an important appointment slipped your mind. Frustration and self-loathing begin to mount. Pause and remind yourself, "I'm a human being. I'm not perfect." Stop beating yourself black and blue. Save your energy to repair the situation as best you can, and go on to have a wonderful day.

Company's about to arrive at just the moment you've chosen to spill a pitcher of iced tea on your new rug. Ordinarily you'd explode in frustration. Not today. Do your (imperfect) best to just let it go and have a good laugh between the tears. Your guests are likely to be amused.

Also, be sure to offer others the same amnesty you are granting yourself. When someone makes a mistake or offends you in some way, be quick to forgive. Perhaps a friend calls you up and begins with "How are you?" only to spend the next half hour talking exclusively about himself. Your irritation gradually builds. Pause. Let go of your grievance. Remember that self-centeredness is a very human failing. Even you, yourself, have occasionally fallen prey to it.

Or you read in the papers about the bloated pronouncements and cynical maneuverings of professional politicians. A surge of anger comes and you think, "If only I were running the country!" The truth is it would probably be in about the same mess. We're all imperfect. Toss away your self-righteous judgmentalism. *That* might start to make a better world.

It can help, as you go through the day or just before bed, to write a list of your mistakes and a second list of the mistakes of others. If so, try to keep the two lists of roughly equal length. If the litany of your faults far outdistances those of others, you may be sinking into self-condemnation. Balance it out by finding a few more screw-ups by those around you; it can help you feel a little better. Conversely, you may be more adept at seeing where others are wrong than at admitting your own mistakes. If so, strive to see when you've been less than perfect. As your ego deflates, your tolerance for others may grow.

To release all these errors symbolically, you might then draw a line through your lists, erase them, or throw them away. On the other hand, you may wish to keep the lists. They're a reminder of our blessed imperfection.

Helpful Hints

The sooner the better. You will find that it's often easier to let go of a grievance if you do so ASAP. You might use a visual image to encourage this. For example, imagine your anger when it starts to build as too much ballast weighing down a ship. Toss it overboard as quickly as possible. Otherwise you may sink.

Or to take an image from author Emmet Fox, see your annoyance as a spark that's just flown onto your shirt. Flick it off quickly and there's no harm done. But wait even a few minutes and what happens? You're burning up. It's much harder to put out a raging fire.

35

Sooner's not always possible. Good intentions notwithstanding, you may find that certain grievances simply can't be flicked off. They've got hooks. You're having difficulty letting go of a hurt, or a mistake you or another person made. Pause. You may need to explore the issue in greater depth, seeking a healing insight. Other games may be helpful, such as #9 "Unpointing the Finger." You might also pray for some divine assistance in being *willing* to forgive.

Forgiveness is a healing circle. Adding power to this game is the notion embodied in the "Lord's Prayer": "Forgive us our trespasses as we forgive those who trespass against us." This healing circle is recognized in many religions. The more we forgive others, the more we open our hearts to the experience of being forgiven.

So when growing angry at another's mistake, you might remember a very similar failing of your own. ("I also have been forgetful, or impatient, or egotistical.") Then hold the two of you together in the light. Ask Spirit for joint forgiveness. It's hard to be self-righteous when you've linked yourself to the other in prayer.

36

Related Readings

Ernest Kurtz and Katherine Ketcham. *The Spirituality of Imperfection.* New York: Bantam Books, 1992. This book focuses on the spiritual need to recognize, accept, work with, even celebrate, our all-too-human flaws.

Harold S. Kushner. *How Good Do We Have to Be?: A New Understanding of Guilt and Forgiveness.* Boston: Little, Brown and Company, 1996. The rabbi rereads classic Bible stories with an emphasis not on sin, but on acceptance and forgiveness.

7. LIFE'S PERFECT LESSONS

You, in fact, are the center of a universe that has been designed perfectly in order to awaken you . . . every experience you have is equally valid as grist for the mill of awakening. . . . This incarnation is the absolute optimal one which you must be in in order to do what needs to be done, or have done through you what needs to be done, in order to bring you home.

—Ram Dass with Stephen Levine, *Grist for the Mill*

When you survey your life, a number of things probably seem askew. Sure, you love your friends and your job is okay. Yet spring allergies may be stringing you out, money worries wearing you down, and a co-worker driving you up a wall. (Feel free to substitute your own list of irritations.) Life would be better, it seems, if only these broken parts could be fixed or discarded.

But what if nothing's broken? The Hindu/Buddhist notion of karma suggests that everything is in your life for a reason. Everything. You've produced present conditions by your actions in the past (which in Eastern thought extends back through many incarnations). But beyond that, the challenges you face are precisely the ones best suited for your spiritual advancement. Your soul has designed for itself the perfect curriculum; it's called your everyday life. This seems hard to believe when stuck at an interminable lunch with Uncle Harry. But according to this view, it's all as it's meant to be, crazy relatives notwithstanding. There are no mistakes.

Today, play your life from this point of view. When challenges and annoyances arise, instead of wishing all was different, ask yourself "What's the lesson here?" Do the same with positive experiences: They're also with you for a reason. Let yourself brainstorm creatively about events.

Perhaps you're embroiled in a dispute with your housemate. It's not just that his cleanliness standards are different than yours. As far as you can tell, *he doesn't have any standards*. Look, instead, for the lesson. This may be an opportunity to let go of control. If you can live and let live with this person, you can do it with anyone. And that would be true freedom.

Or say you've applied for a new job and are still waiting for an answer. And waiting. And waiting. Instead of sitting there willing the phone to ring, pause to view it as a karmic curriculum. Perhaps events are challenging you to become more assertive. Rather than sitting passively, you could call up your prospective employer. On the other hand, there may be lessons in the waiting itself. It's an opportunity to develop patience (not exactly your strong point). Then, too, this waiting may help you be more compassionate of others in a similar position. You might even return those phone messages that have been sitting on your desk for a week.

After brainstorming in such ways, act on any ideas that ring true to you. Practice a little more assertiveness or patience; return your messages, etc. The law of karma suggests the more we absorb and act on lessons now, the less life will force us to repeat them. But don't worry—tomorrow will bring its own teachings. Unless you're a Buddha, you're in no imminent danger of graduating.

You may find it helpful to track this game on paper, for example, with a three-column method. In the first column, note one of the day's events. In the second column, write down any lessons that this event (or person or experience) might have to teach you. You could circle or asterisk those that seem most significant. In a third column, you might note any follow-up actions you take in response, and any shifts that come about as a result.

You might also extend this technique beyond the day's events to issues lingering from the past. Why were you born with a special limitation or talent? Why did you suffer a tragic loss? Note any soul-lessons you've already learned from these conditions, and other things they still have to teach you. If blocked, you can meditate or pray on such matters. Trust that a Divine Teacher will help unveil what you most need to see.

Helpful Hints

You don't have to be Hindu to play. The Eastern notion of karma, and its tie to reincarnation, may seem foreign to your belief system. Still, you're not excluded from the game. After all, its core ideas are present in many traditions, albeit expressed in different terms: that things happen for a reason; that events are shaped by the hand of God; that life tests, purifies, and educates the soul. Even if you're a skeptic, just trying out this perspective can yield insights and constructive responses.

Don't overlook the positive. A good teacher gives the student not just problems and trials, but rewards, incentives, and successes. Life does the same. So be sure to consider the lessons contained in the day's blessings, not just its troubles. To use an earlier example, imagine that after the long wait to hear about a job offer, the call finally arrives: You got it! There may be a teaching here about trusting the universe, or about recognizing your own self-worth. Ponder such lessons while deciding how to spend that newly padded paycheck.

Related Readings

Eknath Easwaran, trans. *The Bhagavad Gita.* Petaluma, CA: Nilgiri Press, 1985. See the author's introduction to this Hindu classic, or any of a number of commentaries on Hinduism or Buddhism, for presentations of the Eastern notion of karma.

Emmet Fox. *The Sermon on the Mount.* San Francisco: HarperSanFrancisco, 1934. Fox argues that the notion of karma is central to Christianity as well: "With what measure ye mete, it shall be measured to you."

8. CHILDREN'S WORLD

But, children, you should never let
Such angry passions rise;
Your little hands were never made
To tear each other's eyes. . . .

Birds in their little nests agree;
And 'tis a shameful sight,
When children of one family
Fall out, and chide, and fight.

—Isaac Watts, *Divine Songs for Children*

gaze about at the adult world. Who can deny it is filled with pettiness and immaturity? Sometimes it seems we're little more than overgrown tykes playing together in the sandbox. Now and then we have fun and share our toys nicely. Other times, we use them to bop each other on the head. We "fall out, and chide, and fight" while God, we might imagine, watches from above, muttering the eternal cry of the parent: "Those kids are driving me crazy! When will they learn to get along?" Yet God witnesses it all, the theologians say, with patience, love, and forgiveness. Maybe we can learn to do so, too.

Today, imagine that all the people you interact with are nothing but big kids. Sure, they've grown in size and sophistication, but each one still houses an inner child. Use this tool not to condemn others ("They're so immature!"), but to better understand and forgive their foibles. After all, we don't expect little children to be perfect. We accept them for who they are.

Say you wake up in the morning to a grumpy spouse. Well, remember, kids are like that when hungry and tired. Wait for the sleepiness to clear and the blood sugar to rise before attempting communication.

Arriving at the office, you find a co-worker in a snit. Don't rush to judgment. Instead, imagine him as a tantruming child. Seek with compassion to understand the cause. Maybe he's frightened. (Is the boss on a rampage?) Perhaps a turn of events left him feeling sad and alone. This can lead kids to act out. Then again, he might be sulking at not getting his way on some office-related matter. Not a very mature response, it's true. But you know that children (including yourself) have a hard time tolerating frustration.

In such ways, practice seeing through the adult façade we all project to the children's world that lies underneath. Use this as a tool not only to forgive the wrongs of others but to celebrate their gifts. Say a friend, Suzanne, calls just to say hi. Imagine her as little Suzy—how nicely she plays with others! Perhaps the check-out person who packs your groceries makes a passing joke. Imagine him as a little child with an impish sense of humor. Pause a moment to join in the fun.

Also, seek to hear what those around you are really asking for behind their grown-up language. Say your partner expresses anger that you're spending too much time with another person. A fight begins to brew sure to include elaborate defenses and counterattacks. Instead, cut to the childlike core. "I want to be loved," your partner is saying. "Don't leave me out. Remember, you're my very best friend." Respond accordingly with a hug, not a harangue.

To track the game in written form, you might use a two-column method. In the first, note some of the "adult" behaviors you witness. In the second column trace each to its childlike motives. You may find that most actions arise from a few simple wishes. For example: wanting to be loved; to be helpful; to have fun; to be included; to grow and learn; to be special; to be secure. Age three or eighty-three—it matters little. We still live in that children's world.

Helpful Hints

Don't forget to have fun. Though this game has a serious purpose, it can also be a source of amusement. Say you have an intimidating boss. Try visualizing him as a small tyke being potty-trained. It's hard to stay quite so afraid. Or see him or her as a kid playing dress-up in that power tie. Come to think of it, isn't everyone in the office, yourself included, simply playing at being grown-ups? Suddenly, the world seems a bit less serious, leaving more room to have fun.

Emulate the loving parent. Certain children, of course, may get on your nerves. After all, it's not *your* child, but somebody else's brat. That's why, in playing this game, it helps not only to see others as children but to view them as a loving parent might. That is, imagine yourself as someone who values, loves, and accepts the child even when he or she's acting out. You can even visualize yourself donning a pair of "god glasses" that helps you see the other through the eyes of a divine Father or Mother.

You too inhabit Children's World. While seeking to share a parent's love, don't forget your own inner child. The same childlike

45

wishes and emotions you find in others are also active in yourself. If you don't remember this, and use it as a tool of self-love, it will be hard to care for those around you.

In this regard, you might look ahead to #11 "The Child Within." You may even wish to play the two games together. They are natural complements.

Related Materials

Big (20th Century-Fox, 1988). This comic movie portrays a young boy magically given a man's body; he navigates the adult world without losing his spirit of play.

A. A. Milne. *Winnie-the-Pooh*. New York: Puffin Books, 1926. This classic can help us recover our sense of a children's world, which even includes depressives (Eeyore), cowards (Piglet), blowhards (Owl), and the simple-minded (Pooh) who, despite their imperfections, take care of each other with love. (Also see the references for #11 "The Child Within.")

9. UNPOINTING the FINGER

It is plain that a life which includes deep resentment leads only to futility and unhappiness. . . . How could we escape? We saw that these resentments must be mastered, but how? . . . Putting out of our minds the wrongs others had done, we resolutely looked for our own mistakes. Where had we been selfish, self-seeking, dishonest and frightened? Though a situation had not been entirely our fault we tried to disregard the other person entirely. Where were we to blame? The inventory was ours, not the other man's.

—Alcoholics Anonymous

~~~

a friend of mind quoted a pithy aphorism: "Whenever I point the finger at another person, there are three fingers pointing back at me." Try it. She has a point. What's more, this image provides a way to help us defuse our lingering resentments.

As you go through the day notice any small angers and frustrations as they start to build. They may be triggered by a waitress who moves too slowly, a co-worker who makes an insensitive remark, or a rambunctious child who won't simmer down. As soon as you're aware of the anger, imagine that you are pointing a finger at the other. Something is wrong and it's clearly his/her/their fault! But now imagine those three other fingers pointing back at you. There's probably some way you, too, are at fault in the situation. If you can find what those fingers are pointing toward, you can better release your anger.

Search out any way that you're in the wrong. Are you responding to the situation impatiently? Are you being too quick to interpret things in the worst possible light? Do the other person's defects remind you of your own? Instead of recognizing this, are you getting stuck in smug self-righteousness? Have you, by actions in the past, contributed to the problem surfacing now? Are you seeking to get something from the other person rather than to give?

In such ways, play the detective. What do those three fingers point toward? As in the process used by Alcoholics Anonymous, it may help to write down some of the reasons you're mad in one column and ways you are at fault in another. You might even draw an outline of a hand, writing these insights into the appropriate fingers.

When you've done this to the best of your ability (it's not always easy), the time has come to let go. Offer acceptance and forgiveness to the other person, and also to yourself. If you need to, pray for the willingness and ability to do so. Then imagine you are unclenching your hand.

Now you're freer to give and receive. If it seems appropriate you might even extend a hand of help or friendship to the other person involved.

Over time you might use this game to search for larger patterns. Who are the prime targets of your anger? What things do you get most resentful about? What seem to be the bedrock causes? What inner or outer changes might you need to make to avoid these repetitive frustrations? Soon you may find you're not unpointing so many fingers. Why? You're not pointing them to begin with.

Helpful Hints

Anticipate emotional resistance. There are many reasons you might resist this game. Perhaps another person has truly done you wrong, and it seems unfair that they "get away with it." You're reluctant to let go of your anger. It also gives you some feeling of power. Then, too, it's no fun to look at where *you're* at fault. Hardly anyone welcomes the process.

Nonetheless, if you stick with it, you may find it freeing, even enjoyable, to search out your flaws. The more you see, the more you become free. After all, your anger is hurting you inside far more than the other person.

Use this as a tool of forgiveness, not self-attack. When you find where you're at fault, it may be tempting to slip into morbid remorse. Instead of beating up the other with an imaginary stick,

49

you end up turning it on yourself. Anger is not dissipated, simply redirected. But remember, that's not the point. We're all imperfect. As important as forgiving another, is to forgive yourself.

Not every resentment will immediately give up the ghost. Let's face it: Some resentments are deeper, tougher, may have lasted for years. We may need recourse to methods beyond this game including intensive prayer, talking with the other, or even radical changes in a relationship. Still, this game can help us start to move beyond blame to seeking constructive solutions.

Related Readings

Alcoholics Anonymous. New York: Alcoholics Anonymous World Services, 1939. This invaluable guide to recovery from alcoholism (equally of use to those with other compulsive problems) gives a spiritually based method for releasing fears, resentments, and character defects.

Harriet Lerner. *Dance of Anger: A Woman's Guide to Changing the Patterns of Intimate Relationships.* New York: HarperCollins, 1989. Anger, the author contends, is not simply toxic, but provides useful information about problems which can be successfully addressed.

10. The FAVORABLE JUDGE

Judging favorably—dan l'kaf zechus—means finding acceptable excuses for questionable behavior, excuses which make sense to us and leave us with a positive feeling towards the other person. It is based on a desire to see the best in others, to recognize their good qualities despite their shortcomings and to attribute worthy intentions to their actions. . . . When we find ourselves suspecting others, we must ask ourselves: Are there any redeeming factors? Did I miss something? Did I jump to the wrong conclusions? . . . Judging favorably means realizing that the other person has his reasons, even if we may disagree with them.

—Yehudis Samet, assisted by Aviva Rappaport,
The Other Side of the Story

"Judging favorably" is recognized in Judaism as a mitzvah (good deed, sacred obligation), prescribed both by the Bible and subsequent rabbinical teachings. Many of us see it as a worthy goal.

Yet how often we practice the opposite! Our mind is quick to convene a court in which others are indicted, prosecuted, and convicted without anything approaching a fair trial. "I left a message on her answering machine three days ago, and she still hasn't returned my call. That's just plain rude! She's no friend of mine."

In this game, let your mental court be presided over by a fair and favorable judge. Whenever a resentment begins to build, make a game of presenting for another the best possible defense. That is, be both the defense attorney and the judge who will arrive at a merciful decision. (If it helps, you might form visual images of these people.) For example, vis-à-vis the accused phone-criminal above: "How do I know she ever got the message I left her? Maybe a family member forgot to give it to her, or the answering machine wasn't working. She may also be really busy this week. Perhaps she hasn't had a moment's free time, or it just slipped her mind amidst all the demands. That's happened to me. It's only human. Plus, even if she did screw up here, I've got to balance this against her good points. She's certainly been a true friend over the years . . ."

In such ways, see if you can acquit the suspect, suspend verdict pending more evidence, or at least reduce your sentence because of mitigating factors.

Apply this method quickly when irritations arise. "That bank clerk is so slow! . . . But I suppose I could learn to slow down myself. Better for my health and sanity." Try it, as well, when you encounter or think of people you habitually find difficult. "My boss is driving me up a wall. But I've got to remember she's got a boss, too, who's probably chewing her out." Just as importantly, do it with yourself. When self-condemnation begins, summon from the wings that same defense attorney and judge, and view yourself favorably.

To make this game more fun, allow yourself to *really get into it.* You've seen those hot lawyers from TV shows and movies who sway juries with ingenious arguments and passion. Do as much. "Yes, ladies and gentlemen of the jury, the plaintiff has been waiting three weeks for his computer, but isn't it a fact that the repair place warned him in advance it might take a while to get the parts? Therefore, *they are not to blame.* Counsel, bring forth the phone records." Pat yourself on the back when you make a particularly telling point.

53

You might also act as court stenographer. Make a list of the people brought up to your mental docket each day. ("My child for throwing a tantrum . . .") In a second column, note your original verdict ("She's a spoiled brat!"), and in a third, the kinder verdict pronounced by the favorable judge ("She's a good kid who just got too tired"). Let the record show that you have conducted your court in the spirit of kindness and truth.

Helpful Hints

No double standards. Sometimes we stand in harsh judgment of others where we'd give ourselves, or our loved ones, a break. We see a poorly parked car that takes up two spaces and think, "WHAT AN IDIOT!" Of course, when we did the same thing once, it was "just a little absent-minded." In such cases, cut the other person slack, as you would for yourself. It's only fair.

Then, too, sometimes a reverse dynamic is at play. You might be more condemning of yourself than anyone else. That's not fair either. Try generously to recognize your good points, and forgive yourself for your mistakes.

You don't have to muzzle the prosecutor. There's a danger that this game will lead you to stuff grievances down into the subconscious where they'll sit and fester. Better to first let accusations emerge: "I can't believe she was so inconsiderate!" After the prosecutor has been allowed his day in court, you may be more able to hear the defense.

Nor need you muzzle others who play the prosecutor. Someone may seek to enlist you in negative gossip: "Can you believe what Jane is doing?!" You need not make that person shut up. This itself can be harsh and judgmental. On the other hand, you needn't join in either, tempting as it may be. Return to the inner voice of the merciful judge before condemning gossiper or gossipee.

The favorable judge is not a fool or do-nothing. You may encounter situations where someone is clearly in the wrong. This game doesn't demand you accept a whitewash, some version of events that's simply untrue. Nor should you tolerate ongoing abuse. This needs to be confronted and corrected.

Still, it's good to hear from the favorable judge before rushing into action. He or she can help us acknowledge mitigating factors, hear the other side, and not become too self-righteous. Then our intervention is more likely to be compassionate and effective.

55

Related Readings

Thich Nhat Hanh. *The Heart of Understanding.* Berkeley, CA: Parallax Press, 1978. This commentary on an ancient Buddhist text stresses the import of empathic understanding even of those we ordinarily reject.

Yehudis Samet, assisted by Aviva Rappaport. *The Other Side of the Story.* New York: Mesorah Publications, 1996. A rich and detailed volume of pointers for how to play the favorable judge.

Part Three

LOVING the SELF

h aving traveled the path of acceptance and forgiveness, we arrive at the gates of love. We may find them, however, guarded by a dragon that blocks our immediate entrance. This dragon goes by many names: low self-esteem, lack of self-confidence, and in its extreme forms, blatant self-hate. The Bible enjoins us to "love thy neighbor as thyself." But we cannot begin to fulfill this commandment if we lack healthy self-love. As Rabbi Joshua Liebman writes, "The fact is that we often treat ourselves more rigidly, more fanatically, more vengefully than we do others. . . . He who hates himself, who does not have proper regard for his own capacities, powers, compassions, actually can have no respect for others. Deep within himself he will hate his brothers when he sees in them his own marred image."

So before we can care for others, we must learn to love the self. This is true, as well, for another reason: Without self-acceptance, we're like empty vessels always seeking to be filled from another's cup. Even when we do good, there will be a hidden agenda based more on getting than on giving—"see how good I am, think well of me, love me please." Yet no approval seems quite enough to fill the cup. It's always leaking from a hole in the center.

Healthy self-regard plugs that hole and fills us from within. We're better able to see the good in self, to take care of our own needs, and to perceive and accept Divine love. Filled up in this way, our cup naturally spills over into love of other people and God.

Yet, can we love ourselves in the face of our faults? "I'm such a worrier. It drives people crazy. Plus, I'm impatient. Half the time I want to kick the dog and yell at my kids, or vice-versa. Holy people don't think like that." Yes, but human beings do on their way to becoming holy. Even saints struggle with their sins. In the words of Buddha, "You can search throughout the entire universe for someone who is more deserving of your love and affection than you are yourself, and that person is not to be found anywhere. You yourself, as much as anybody in the entire universe, deserve your love and affection."

This is an attitude that must be worked at (or played at) as much as any other in the spiritual life. The following games are designed to help. They're about caring for the self, including parts we sometimes want to throw away like the "shadow" or the "inner child." They're about nursing our wounds; setting proper boundaries; finding shelter from life's storms. To care for ourselves thusly is no selfish enterprise. Surely it's the will of a loving God concerned with our well-being.

11. The CHILD WiTHiN

The process of living, of coming alive, is a process of
befriending the self. We need to love our inner child—all those
hurt, scared, sad, and angry places. When we bring love and for-
giveness to that child we transform childish attitudes and become
more childlike. To be like a child is to be delighted with the world,
curious and unafraid to take risks, eager to grow and learn.

—Diane Mariechild, *Open Mind: Women's Daily Inspiration*
for Becoming Mindful

oday, imagine that you have within you the soul of a small child. This child is none other than you, yourself, as you were at a younger age. How young? This is something for you to discover. Your child may be two, four, seven years old. Sense the age that most seeks expression.

As you go through the day, interact with that child in a number of healing ways. First, pause frequently to ask, "How are you doing?" If all you're engaged in is work, work, work, you may encounter a grumpy kid. "What about time for play?!" Or if someone behaved in a slighting fashion, that child may be feeling hurt. Perhaps a co-worker barely paused to say hello. You, as an adult, know it's no big deal. She was simply preoccupied. But the inner child is sensitive to rejection. "No one likes me. No one wants to be my friend." Don't shut off this voice and the feelings expressed. In order to heal, you first must feel.

A next step is to ask that child what would help him or her to feel comforted, well cared for, happy. That grumpy, overworked kid may want a break. "For a few minutes, let's just play a silly computer game." Or perhaps that child who feels so friendless needs a kind word and a hug. Tell him or her, "You're a wonderful kid." Imagine yourself wrapping your arms around the child, or visualize a divine being doing the same. Let that child climb up into God's lap and relax.

This game is not just about healing a wounded child. The inner child can also be a messenger of joy to heal the wounded adult. Asking the child, "What would make you happy?" may unlock your hidden desires. "I want to go to lunch today at that outdoor cafe." "I want to hear my favorite song, the one that makes me cry." Or "Let's just sit here and watch raindrops. They run down the windowpane like they're in a race. Let's bet on which gets to the bottom first." Reawaken some of the magic and wonder that you lost touch with as you "matured."

Not everything the child feels should be outwardly expressed. He or she may be prone to fits of selfishness and rage. And not everything the child wants to do is wise or even feasible. "Let's leave work. I want ice cream right now." Unfortunately, it's 11:00 A.M. on a Wednesday. Your boss isn't paying you to indulge every wish. So another part of the game is to set appropriate limits for your inner child. Having recognized certain desires, you may need to rein them in or postpone. But like a good parent, you can explain this to yourself with sensitivity. "I know you're angry. That's okay. You can even stomp your foot, hit a pillow. But it's not okay to hurt someone, or to hurt yourself." Or "I know you want to play now. But first we have to work. As soon as work's over, then we'll go get some ice cream." Your child will flourish with appropriate limits based on principles of love.

You might also communicate with your child through writing. Ask questions and let the child pen a response. Consider writing with your nondominant hand (the left, if you're a righty). It's surprising what thoughts and feelings this can release.

As any parent knows, young children thrive on routines. Special treats are great, but more important are the basics: getting enough sleep, eating nutrituous food, finding that balance between hard activity and restful play.

Use this game to discern the patterns that are healthy for you. If your child is dragging, hear the message that you may need more sleep than you currently permit yourself. If your blood-sugar level drops precipitously midafternoon, and with it your energy, patience, and mood, build in an afternoon snack. Let the child within teach you how to be a more happy and effective adult.

Helpful Hints

View your inner child as a loving parent might. It can be surprisingly hard to take care of yourself, especially when you're less than perfect. Feelings of guilt, impatience, and self-hatred may interfere: "You've done a stupid thing. You've screwed it all up." If you struggle with such thoughts, use this game to view yourself anew. What if this "kid" weren't you, but your own son or daughter? It might not be easy, but wouldn't you do your best to be a good parent? To understand, to forgive, and to help? Try to draw on the best of any experience you have had as a parent or caregiver, as well as good examples you've witnessed from others. As best you can, be that loving parent to yourself.

Ask for spiritual help. Even following the above advice, it's hard to always know how to care for your child appropriately. The models provided by your own parents may have been flawed. All the more reason to seek help beyond the human sphere. You can image a Father/Mother imbued with infinite love and wisdom. Ask for inspiration as to how best to nurture your child. Listen for intuitive guidance.

Even then, problems may arise beyond your power to fix. For example, your child (that is, you) may be plagued by fears or grief

63

that you cannot simply will away. Again, let a Higher Power help. It's much easier to face troubles when clutching the hand of the Divine.

Receive spiritual help from your child. As Father and Mother are archetypal images of God, so, too, is that of the Child. In many religions, a "wonder-child" (for example, the baby Jesus) expresses the innocence and joy of Spirit. So God can get involved in this game from another angle: through the voice of that child within. Let him or her speak to you of your soul-level yearnings; of life abundant; of childlike trust.

Related Readings

John Bradshaw. *Homecoming: Reclaiming and Championing Your Inner Child.* New York: Bantam Books, 1990. A set of principles and techniques for how to heal the wounds of the inner child that can linger throughout adulthood.

Frances Hodgson Burnett. *The Secret Garden.* New York: HarperCollins, 1911. This classic book, wonderful for kids and adults alike, tells the story of two children who are abandoned and emotionally stunted, yet who help each other blossom into the fullness of life.

12. KISSING the BOO-BOO

A devotee asked the Master, "By what means can [God] be seen?" and the Master replied: "Can you weep for Him with intense longing?" . . . So long as a child is engrossed in play with its toys, the mother engages herself in cooking and other household works. But when the little one finds no more satisfaction in toys, throws them aside and loudly cries for its mother, she can no longer remain in the kitchen. She perhaps drops down the rice pot from the hearth, and runs in hot haste to the child and takes it up in her arms.

—*Sayings of Sri Ramakrishna*

a s you go through the day, you will doubtlessly experience your quota of minor injuries. Maybe you're tired from a late night out; hurt by a friend's snub; disappointed by some turn of events. We're used to shaking off these small "slings and arrows of outrageous fortune" and getting on with the day. "I'm fine." But wounds that are left untreated can fester, causing even more damage in the end.

This game extends the principles of the previous, "The Child Within," into a specific healing technique. Today, when you suffer a hurt or disappointment, put it through a TRIPLE-A treatment regimen. First, pause to *acknowledge* the hurt. Even if you think it's a small, stupid issue (what do I care if a store clerk treats me rudely?), the fact is the event caused you pain. Second, *ask* for healing. As in Sri Ramakrishna's story, imagine a loving God or Goddess, or any other spiritual being, ready to care for you. See yourself as a toddler who runs immediately to mommy or daddy to have the "boo-boo" kissed.

Third, *accept* the kiss. That is, cooperate with Spirit in offering yourself and implementing whatever care you need. Played out from the day's frenetic pace? Climb into a soothing bubble bath. The mailman delivered a rejection slip? Spend a few minutes remembering your successes. Missing an old friend who moved to another city? It can help just to sit quietly with the grief. Each of these is a boo-boo that needs to be recognized and kissed.

To track this game, you might make two columns on a page, one called Boo-Boos, the other (what else?) Kisses. Note the day's small hurts and healings. It may take time to discover the sorts of kisses you most need, so be willing to experiment. Dealing with sadness? Try a cup of tea. Or a piece of favorite music. Or curling up on the couch with a soft blanket and a good book. Find out what best turns the trick.

Kissing the boo-boo might not be testable on a double-blind trial of medications. But don't tell that to the child who feels loved and taken care of, and therefore begins to heal. Can't we use the same, even though we're now the grown-ups? Ask for and accept those kisses.

Helpful Hints

Trust your way to God. Part of what heals the child is the faith that he or she places in the kiss. Similarly, trust that a divine force will salve your wounds by providing love and guidance. Access this help in whatever way works for you: prayer, visualization, intuitive thoughts. Your boo-boos may be a powerful way to deepen your connection with Spirit.

Cooperate with self-love. Many a frustrated parent has told many a child: "I can't help you if you don't cooperate." Similarly, you need to cooperate with this game by adopting self-loving attitudes. You might not always wish to. You may feel that your pain is the consequence of your blunders, or even punishment well-deserved. But this is not how a loving parent views matters. First the boo-boo needs to be treated. Later there will be time to consider changes that might prevent boo-boos of the future.

Be okay with not being okay. You may find that the "kisses" don't fully relieve the hurt. This can be frustrating. Then the thought may come, "I'm failing at the game." Of course, this merely makes the boo-boo worse.

Instead, be okay with not being okay. Recognize that sadness, loss, disappointment, fear, and anger (to name just a few) are part of the human repertoire and sometimes unavoidable. This acceptance can itself be healing. Sometimes it's the best kiss our boo-boo can receive.

Related Readings

Joan Borysenko. *Guilt is the Teacher, Love is the Lesson.* New York: Warner Books, 1990. The author speaks to our healing from self-defeating voices of guilt and shame. (Also see the readings for the previous game, "The Child Within.")

Pema Chödrön. *Awakening Loving-Kindness.* Boston: Shambhala, 1991. A Buddhist nun emphasizes the importance of being gentle with the self while on a spiritual path.

13. The AFFIRMATIVE No

We have seen and known people who seem to have found this deep Center of living, where the fretful calls of life are integrated, where no as well as yes can be said with confidence. We've seen such lives, integrated, unworried by the tangles of close decisions, unhurried, cheery, fresh, positive. . . . Much of our acceptance of multitudes of obligations is due to our inability to say no. . . . But when we say yes or no to calls, on the basis of inner guidance and whispered promptings of encouragement from the Center of our life, or on the basis of a lack of any inward "rising" of that Life to encourage us in the call, we have no reason to give, except one—the will of God as we discern it. Then we have begun to live in guidance. And I find he never guides us into an intolerable scramble of panting feverishness.

—Thomas R. Kelly, *A Testament of Devotion*

*l*ife can sometimes seem like a hurried mess. Demands press upon us from every direction. There are chores to be done, organizations to join, projects to complete, requests to fulfill. These usurp our time and energy until little is left for the things we most care about. In a garden chock full of weeds, the flowers will inevitably suffer. So, too, will our capacity for joy and peace in the midst of an overstuffed life.

Today, practice saying no. "No," used properly, can be a most affirmative word; it clears space to say "Yes!" to something else. We are weeding the garden to make room for the flowers that are truly meant to flourish.

Say someone calls you in the morning while you're minding your kid. "Can you talk now?" Ordinarily you'd say "Of course," not wanting to offend. Today, pause to think or pray before you respond. Maybe the proper answer is, "No, I'll call you back a little later." Each time you say no to something, think what other thing this enables you to say yes to, such as, "giving my child undivided attention; feeling more peaceful inside; being more present to my friend when we talk later." It might help to write down your nos in one column, and in a second column, the yeses these permit.

70

Sometimes a clear and simple no is best. "No, I don't want to go to the movies tonight." (Yes to a quiet evening, and early to bed.) Or sometimes the best no is a partial one. "I'll write the report, but I can't get it to you by Tuesday. How about Thursday at the latest?" (Yes to feeling saner, plus doing a better job.)

At times we serve as our own taskmasters, harsher than anyone else. So use the affirmative no not only with others, but also with yourself. Your mind may generate pressures, worries, resentments, and fears.

Today, don't be a passive consumer. Say no to unwanted thoughts. Clear a space for the experience you are meant to have. "No, even though I think it's filthy, I don't have to wash the kitchen floor tonight. More important to let myself relax." Or, "No, I don't want to get all anxious about the party we're hosting. It'll go fine. I choose to think positive."

The affirmative no can be hard to do. If you find it so, you might explore in thought or writing why this is the case. Are you afraid of displeasing others? Does low self-esteem leave you feeling unworthy to set boundaries? Without judging yourself, see whatever you see. This game, and others in the book, may provide some help with these issues.

The more we practice the affirmative no, a curious thing occurs: Our yes becomes more sincere. If we say yes to a request from outside or within, we're no longer doing it from fear or force of habit. We really mean it. It's a flower we want to plant in our garden, not just another weed.

So, today, when appropriate, also use the affirmative yes. "Yes, I will come to that committee meeting. It's important I be there." Or, "Yes, I will make dinner tonight. I actually feel like cooking." Then go at these things with zest and energy. You're saying yes to life.

Helpful Hints

Take a "nos break." Your life probably includes a number of obligatory duties. You can't exactly say no to setting your alarm, going to work in the morning, and a host of other duties. But how you approach these activities is more under your control. Choose the experience you wish to have.

A simple technique may help. Every hour, on the hour, some radio stations take a newsbreak. Consider instead pausing each hour (a watch beeper comes in handy) to take a "nos break." That is, stop to ask yourself, "Right now, what do I most want to say no to?" (for example, mounting stress, self-pity, procrastination, or boredom). Then ask, "What do I want to say yes to?" In this way, keep rechoosing your experience.

Don't apologize. When saying an affirmative no, you may feel you must weave a web of defenses, justifications, and apologies. "I'm sorry, I'd love to have lunch, but not on Wednesday, because my mother is in town, and I have a dentist appointment, plus a major presentation at work coming up. I appreciate being asked. Believe me, I'm not trying to put you off." Actually, such apologies can be more off-putting than a simple refusal. To coin a phrase, *just say no.* Or, if appropriate, append a brief explanation: "This week is all scheduled up." But don't feel you have to justify every no to another's satisfaction. What's important is that *you* believe it's justified.

Use the "affirmative maybe." When someone requests something of you it may be hard to discern immediately the best response. Often, commitments made in haste are regretted at leisure. ("Why did I say I'd fill in on Saturday? . . . That sure was dumb!") So give yourself some time. When a request is made, dare to respond, "Let me think about it. I'll give you a call." For the moment, leave it at "maybe." This allows you to consider your options before you arrive at a decision.

73

Seek guidance. The quote from Thomas Kelly stresses how our nos and yeses can flow from a sense of God's will. Whatever terms you use, seeking such spiritual guidance can help immeasurably with this game. "What am I meant to do? Where can I best exercise my talents? What would foster harmony and balance here? What gives me the most joy? What is the will of a loving God?" Such questions, voiced in prayer and meditation, can assist us to make proper choices. They're more likely to be grounded in the depths of Spirit rather than surface concerns.

Related Readings

Janet Luhrs. *The Simple Living Guide: A Sourcebook for Less Stressful, More Joyful Living.* New York: Broadway Books, 1997. Practicing the affirmative no can help lead us to a simpler life.

Manuel J. Smith. *When I Say No, I Feel Guilty.* New York: Bantam Books, 1975. While not spiritual in focus, this is a helpful guide to proper assertiveness, especially useful for those who find saying no a struggle.

14. SEEING YOUR SHADOW

One of the most important aspects of healing ourselves and the earth is the willingness to face our "shadow"—the feelings and parts of ourselves that we have rejected, repressed, or disowned. Our society has tremendous prohibitions against feeling too much. We are afraid to feel too much fear, hurt, sadness, or anger, and oftentimes we are also afraid to feel too much love, passion, or joy! And we're definitely afraid of our natural sensuality and sexuality. . . . As we begin to accept them as vital parts of ourselves, we begin to find safe, constructive modes of expression. . . . Through integrating all aspects of ourselves, we become whole.

—Shakti Gawain, *Return to the Garden: A Journey of Discovery*

"**i** have a little shadow that goes in and out with me." The truth of this nursery rhyme extends to the notion of the "shadow" advanced by psychiatrist C. G. Jung. In the light of day we present the person we would like to be: kind, competent, friendly (fill in your own terms). But we are shadowed by all those other parts of the self that we've been taught to conceal and reject. This shadow, Jung taught, varies from person to person, but can include elements of rage, lust, egocentrism, or other forbidden emotions and desires.

Unrecognized and unaccepted, the shadow can do harm. We feel guilty for our subconscious "evil" impulses. To evade self-blame, we then project our shadow onto others. "Robert is so self-centered, not me." The result can be prejudice and conflict, even on a global scale. "Those people (of a certain race, nationality, or religion) are obviously inferior!" We cannot love others or ourselves until we accept our own shadow.

To unfold, any shadow needs space. So this game will employ the letters SPACE as its mnemonic.

SP stands for *SPotting* the shadow. As you go through the day, try to spot those forbidden thoughts, feelings, and wishes you often hide from yourself. Perhaps you notice you're becoming a little agitated, and are not sure why. Quick, look for the shadow. Bring it into the light of awareness. Maybe it's "I want everyone to pay attention to me, and they're not!" Or, "I'm feeling really depressed and sad today." Or, "I'm about ready to put this kid out for the trash collectors!"

The A in SPACE stands for the next step—*Accepting* whatever you've seen. Initially, you may be frightened by your shadow-thoughts, or feel they're dirty and bad. But remember, everyone's got a shadow. Remind yourself that these wishes and feelings are human, all-too-human. (Who doesn't get mad at their kids?) It would be wrong to act on certain wishes in ways destructive to self or others. But the more you accept your shadow, the more you can channel its energy in healthy ways.

This is the CE of our SPACE mnemonic—the search for *Creative Expression.* Our shadow thoughts and wishes often contain seeds of rich vitality that can help to make us whole. The trick is to express this material creatively, not destructively. Don't put that kid out for the trash collectors, but do seek some healthy expression of your feelings rather than just pushing them away.

This can take many different forms. Using anger at your child as an example, maybe it's enough simply to run with your fantasy, and laugh at it within. You might write about it in a journal, or shape it into a poem. Then, too, you can share your frustration in prayer, and seek help from your Higher Power. Or maybe you need to talk with your partner who might be having similar feelings. You'll get through it better together.

Or you might need an outlet for your aggression. Consider going for a run, putting loud music on the headphones, or pounding on a pillow. You can be more loving and patient after this release.

Then, too, your anger may signal something that needs to be changed. Perhaps you should speak more directly to your child about whatever behavior is so aggravating. Or maybe *you* need to shift inside— lighten up and be less controlling. Then again, maybe the two of you just need more time apart. Absence can make the heart grow fonder.

In such ways, try to give your shadow healing *space* by *spotting* it, *accepting* it, and allowing it *creative expression*. You "have a little shadow that goes in and out" with you. So why not make it your friend?

Helpful Hints

See your shadow in others. Often your judgments of others can help you spot your own shadow. Notice if there's someone who particularly gets on your nerves. "That Jack, he's an attention-seeking baboon!" Or you may be quick to condemn some group, implicitly flattering yourself by comparison. "Politicians are a bunch of self-serving, money-grubbing twits!" Well, true or not, it may be that what you're condemning so vehemently is your own repressed shadow. Maybe you, like most humans given the right conditions, can also be attention-seeking, self-serving, and money-grubbing. It's easier to project these qualities onto others, but seeing them in yourself can help your hostility melt.

Get to know your shadow. Over time, your spottings may allow you to sketch a composite picture of your shadow. Are you most prone to disown your angry and aggressive feelings? Your sexuality? Your jealousies? Your sadness, or your childlike joys? Seek to know the personality (or many personalities) of your shadow.

You might also think about its origins. For example, were there certain messages you received as a child about "nice" girls or boys that led you to deny certain impulses? But remember, you're seeking self-knowledge here, not to blame others. After all, they too had their own shadows.

Be patient with yourself and seek spiritual help. Be forewarned: This game is a challenging one. You might recognize some disturbing impulses you find hard to accept. Or you might choose some manner of creative expression that in retrospect you judge destructive. "I tried to explain my feelings to my husband but he got angry and distant. Maybe I should have just kept my mouth shut."

Maybe, maybe not. Accept that you are exploring uncharted territory. Now and then you may feel lost or stumble, and others may become distressed at your explorations. That's okay. We learn through trial and error. Be patient with yourself and with others' reactions.

But it can also be useful to seek aid from a Higher Power who already knows you through and through. "Help me to acknowledge my shadow-side. To accept it, laugh at it, dance with it. To see how best to express what I'm feeling. In this situation, what would be healthy and life-giving, not destructive?" Through such prayer and meditation, you may receive the guidance you need.

Related Readings

Robert Bly. *A Little Book on the Human Shadow.* San Francisco: HarperSanFrancisco, 1988. Just as the title says, by a noted contemporary poet and essayist.

Robert A. Johnson. *Owning Your Own Shadow: Understanding the Dark Side of the Psyche.* San Francisco: HarperSanFrancisco, 1990. A Jungian analyst explores the task of understanding and honoring the shadow.

Thomas Moore. *Care of the Soul.* New York: HarperPerennial, 1992. A rich discussion of the need to accept our wounds, symptoms, and shadow-side, if we are to cultivate the richness of soul.

15. HOME SWEET HOME

There was once a man who had two sons; and the younger said to his father, "Father, give me my share of the property." So he divided his estate between them. A few days later the younger son turned the whole of his share into cash and left home for a distant country, where he squandered it in reckless living. . . . Then he came to his senses and said, "How many of my father's paid servants have more food than they can eat, and here am I, starving to death." . . . So he set out for his father's house. But while he was still a long way off his father saw him, and his heart went out to him. He ran to meet him, flung his arms round him and kissed him. . . . Now the elder son was out on the farm; and on his way back, as he approached the house, he heard music and dancing. . . . The servant told him, "Your brother has come home, and your father has killed the fatted calf because he has him back safe and sound." But he was angry and refused to go in. His father came out and pleaded with him; but he retorted, "You know how I slaved for you all these years; I never once disobeyed your orders; and you never gave me so much as a kid, for a feast with my friends." . . . "My boy," said the father, "you are always with me, and everything I have is yours. How could we help celebrating his happy day? Your brother here was dead and has come back to life, was lost and is found."

— Luke 15:11–32

This well-known parable of the prodigal son may be read as an allegory of the spiritual life. The father's house can represent that place within our heart where we rest when spiritually centered. At such times we experience a sense of love, peace, or comfort that tells us we have truly "come home."

The notion of a spiritual home is not particular to Christianity. Associated with the Temple in Jerusalem, Jewish scripture celebrates the "house of the Lord" (for example, see the 23rd or 27th Psalm). There one finds goodness and mercy, joy and safety. Similar imagery can be found in other traditions, testifying to its universality. We all know what it feels like to be a stranger in a strange land, and the comfort of coming home.

Begin today's game by drawing aside for a few minutes, growing quiet, and visualizing, in your mind's eye, your own spiritual home. Feel free to imagine it however you will. Do you see a glorious palace, a cozy little house, or a bare monastery? Is it similar to any place you've ever lived or visited? Where is it situated—on a mountaintop or near the ocean; deep in a forest or ringed by gardens? How many rooms does this home have? Is one set aside just for you, and, if so, how is it furnished? And who, if anyone, resides there with you? Spiritual beings, special loved ones, all of humankind? Don't let your rational mind or theological models dictate such matters. Instead, let your intuitive heart transport you to a place where you feel loved and secure. To make this place more vivid, you may wish at some point to paint an image of it, or write about it in your journal.

Today, wherever duty takes you—on a commute to work, or bustling through the mall—resolve to stay at home. That is, pause periodically to visualize the spiritual home you imagined, and use this image to remain centered.

This may not be easy in the face of life's challenges. Say a fight breaks out between you and your partner. Or, more dramatically, a call arrives to inform you an old friend has died. Instead of spinning out, you can use your spiritual home as a place to work through such things. Imagine yourself and your partner there. Envisioning peace restored, you can manifest this better in your demeanor. Or visualize yourself with that friend who died, walking hand-in-hand through the garden. Say what needs to be said. Let the tears come. You can do that in your spiritual home.

As much as you resolve to stay home during the day, expect to wander off time and again. Perhaps things are stressful at work. Or the phone doesn't stop ringing with annoying solicitations: "Do you currently receive the *Times-Picayune*? Can you tell me why not?" Soon you find yourself journeying far from home in a wasteland of jangled nerves.

As soon as you notice you're not at home, stop. Reflect for a minute on what has caused you to depart. Are you more like the younger child, living heedless of Spirit, caught up in the seductions of daily life? He "left home for a distant country." In writing, you might note the particular "distant countries" you run off to. ("Rushing, worrying, overeating . . .") Or are you like the elder, banished by his own self-righteousness? You might note such elder-brother judgmental attitudes that also pull you away from home. ("I want to *execute* those phone solicitors.")

Regardless, imitate the child who "came to his senses." The most important thing is not to win an argument, rush through tasks, or punish a wrongdoer, but to get your butt back home.

Imagine yourself letting go of negative stuff like so much useless baggage. As best you can, drop these attitudes, or ask Spirit to take them away. Return mentally to that spiritual house you visualized. See again its courtyards and furnishings. If there's anything that must be worked through, do it there. Remember the words of that cinematic sage, Dorothy: "There's no place like home." Home is where you belong.

Helpful Hints

Nothing wrong with a little redesigning. You may find that your vision of your spiritual home changes over time. Its entire shape or location may alter in surprising ways. Perhaps you discover new rooms and courtyards in which you meet new friends. If so, that's fine. The changing needs of your soul may best be served by these changes. And you don't even have to pay a contractor.

It's a great place to meet your maker. Other games in this book involve imagined conversations with God, a wise elder, or other spiritual friends. Why not hold these meetings in your spiritual home? Visualize the scene as vividly as you can. See yourself sitting down to a tea and muffin with Jesus or Buddha. Or you might imagine yourself wandering in the garden with God (just don't pick any apples). Such images can enrich your prayer-life.

Two sons in one? When you feel far from home spiritually (like the younger son), thoughts of self-condemnation may arise. "You brought it on yourself, you fool!" This is the voice of the elder son, aching to spoil your return. At such times it's good to remember the father's love: "He ran to meet [the younger son], flung his arms round him and kissed him." Know that God or Spirit embraces you in this way, and be willing to embrace yourself.

Related Readings

Jann Mitchell. *Home Sweeter Home: Creating a Haven of Simplicity and Spirit*. Hillsboro, OR: Beyond Words Publishing, 1996. Suggestions for how to turn your actual home and homelife into a nurturing sanctuary.

Henri J. M. Nouwen. *The Return of the Prodigal Son*. New York: Doubleday, 1992. A wonderful book on this gospel story and the painting of it by Rembrandt, with a focus on homecoming and reconciliation.

St. Theresa of Avila. *Interior Castle*. Garden City, NY: Image Books, 1961. In this classic of mysticism, Theresa portrays the soul as an interior castle with "many mansions" we advance through in our quest for the Divine. (In a more contemporary vein, see Max Lucado's *The Great House of God: A Home for Your Heart*.)

Part Four
The Generous
Heart

t he previous set of games focused on self-love. When our cup is filled from within, I said, it overflows into love of others. But let's be honest: It's also human to be selfish and self-centered. "*My* cup, *my* liquid, I don't want to give it away. Maybe there won't be enough left for me." Sometimes we feel this way about money, time, approval, you name it. The same feelings can arise even on the spiritual quest. In the words of Gampopo, 12th century Tibetan teacher, "Unless the mind be trained to selflessness and infinite compassion, one is apt to fall into the error of seeking liberation for self alone."

Yet self-centeredness does not yield true freedom. It tends to place us into conflict with others, and breeds loneliness and fear. We don't feel whole, but separated from those around us and from the Spirit who loves us all. Or as the mystics claim, who *is* us all.

We thus encounter a paradox. We best refill our own cup when we pour love out to others. Giving blesses best the giver.

"Yes, yes, all well and good, this love-thy-neighbor stuff, especially if you're a Mother Teresa. But I'm just not built that way. I'm hardly the soul of compassion. I can be judgmental, uncaring, and greedy." Yes, again that's part of being human. But so is the capacity for growth. In the words of Buddhist teacher Sharon Salzberg, "Love and concern for all are not things some of us are born with and others are not. . . . We can choose to transform our minds so that they embody love, or we can allow them to develop habits and false concepts of separation." The culture we live in reinforces the latter. Personal success is all the rage. But the world's religions suggest we practice love and service. Finally, the choice rests with each of us.

We may hesitate if we associate service only with self-sacrifice and pain. It's true that love can be hard work; there are times we must put our wishes aside to meet another's needs. But the games in this section reveal another side. Giving can also be great fun. It lifts us out of self, provides a sense of purpose, stimulates creativity and closeness. Soon we're not sure if we're doing it to bring joy to others or to ourselves. That very distinction starts to drop away as we taste of our unity.

But whether this is so depends on the spirit behind our giving. Does it express genuine care or just a guilt-ridden sense of duty? Are we truly seeking to make others happy or simply to show off our virtues? Does helping draw us closer to others? Or does it leave us feeling better than (or worse than) those we serve?

To avoid potential hazards, these games focus on cultivating the generous heart. Helping arises naturally from respect and compassion for others. Over time, service becomes a habit of being. It's not so much something we *do* with great fanfare; it's just a part of who we *are*.

16. WLUV

Just as a mother, with her own life, protects her only child from hurt,
So with a boundless heart should you cherish all living beings.
Radiate loving-kindness over the whole world, spreading upward to
the skies, and
downward to the depths,
Unrestrained, free from hate and ill will.

Standing or walking, sitting or lying down,
During all your waking hours,
Devote your mind and heart to this;
It is known as the life divine.

—*The Buddha, selection from the Sutta-Nipata*

Central to Buddhism is the "*metta*" meditation, or meditation on loving-kindness. The spiritual aspirant sends thoughts of love and benevolence to an ever-widening circle of beings. The game presented here links this age-old practice to an image based on modern technology.

Pretend there's a radio station inside your head. Its call letters are WLUV (or KLUV if you live out west). Any radio station has its own format, whether classic rock, rap music, talk show, or easy listening. WLUV also sticks to a consistent theme. It broadcasts only good wishes and loving thoughts. Sure, there are other stations in your head sending out complaints, fears, and criticisms. But today you're listening to the all-love station, WLUV.

Early in the day, switch to this station in the following way. Call to mind a scene when you were feeling real love for another. Maybe you were bouncing your child on your knee, or embracing your partner, or even frolicking with your dog. Whatever image comes, take a few moments to let it fill your heart with love-energy. WLUV is gathering its megawatts, ready to come on the air.

Now begin broadcasting. Translate that energy into three positive wishes for the other you visualized. "May my daughter Sarah be happy. May Sarah be free from suffering. May Sarah experience peace." You can choose any phrases that embody your love, but keep them short and sweet.

Having sent love to this being, now do so toward yourself. "May I be happy. May I be free from suffering. May I experience peace." (Or, if it feels more comfortable, insert your name.) The more love you generate toward yourself, the more you'll have to radiate to others.

Next, think of a "neutral person," someone for whom you have neither positive nor negative feelings. This might be a co-worker or casual acquaintance. Broadcast to them the same well-wishes. Then do so with someone you do not like, or with whom you're in the midst of a conflict. WLUV does not discriminate. Its signal spreads out through the airwaves (mind-waves) equally to all. In this spirit, finish the session by directing your three good wishes to a much larger group around you—such as everyone in your company, city, country, or even to all living beings. Sense WLUV's powerful worldwide transmission.

Though you've completed one "talk show," know that WLUV will be on the air all day. It's up to you how often to tune in. You can do so by sending messages of love to anyone you think of or meet. Perhaps you notice an office assistant who looks unusually harried. Pause to think: "May Sheila be joyful. May Sheila be free of worry. May Sheila know she is loved." You can stick with your original blessings, or alter them to fit the situation.

It may be especially helpful to play this game when your thoughts take a negative turn. Perhaps you've grown harshly critical of yourself or another person. Just imagine this as some other radio station—perhaps WYUK. It features those shock-jocks who love to slice people up. Those stations can be titillating for awhile, but are hardly healthy as constant mental fare. Gently readjust your dial. Recall that tender scene you imaged in the morning to get some love-energy back. Then send your well-wishes to whomever, moments before, was under attack. There it is, you've located the signal again—WLUV.

While you're at it, you might imagine your whole mind as a radio-dial. In addition to WLUV, how many different stations can you identify? For example, is there a WORY, broadcasting fears twenty-four hours a day? Is there a KVCH (kvetch!)—all-complaint radio, all the time? Make up your own call letters. Playfully imagine the sort of disk jockeys, special shows, and ads each station would employ. You might even draw a diagram of this radio dial, every station assigned its place.

Then as you go through the day notice how much time you spend listening to each. Are you tuning in more to WYUK or WLUV? Over time, see if you can't grow more selective. After all, the radio is owned and operated by you.

Helpful Hints

It's okay to vary WLUV's programming. In this game you employ a series of repeated blessings. Over time, you might find the reiteration of the same words a bit deadening, encouraging you to tune out. If so, feel free to vary your broadcasting as long as it's consistent with WLUV's basic theme. That is, generate thoughts of compassion, sympathetic judgments, and positive wishes. You might even play songs like "Dedicated to the One I Love." If it helps, you can imagine God as WLUV's program manager, throwing novel ideas your way.

Frustrated? Bored? Tune in. Tuning into WLUV can enrich situations that otherwise might be frustrating or mundane. Stuck on a long bus ride? You might think of all your friends or family members and, one by one, send them love. Or you can even WLUV the other bus passengers. Look into each person's face. Say an old man sits across from you: Try to see with compassion the suffering he may have endured; the uniqueness of his personality; the same desire for happiness that he shares with all people. Send him a blessing before moving on to the next person. And when you get off the bus, take a WLUV walk. Broadcast your good wishes to each stranger you pass. Suddenly they won't seem so strange.

WLUV is a fledgling station in need of your support. You might become discouraged when your attempts to broadcast love seem feeble and insincere. Perhaps you repeat your phrases but without much genuine feeling, especially in relation to those you dislike. At other times you might forget (or refuse) to tune in for hours. Don't despair. Remember that you're just getting WLUV up and running. It may not yet have the most powerful signal, or top the rating charts. But the more you broadcast, the more WLUV gathers wattage. Over time, it will come in loud and clear.

Related Readings

Ann Lamott. *Bird by Bird: Some Instructions on Writing and Life*. New York: Pantheon Books, 1994. In this engaging book on the art and spirit of writing, Lamott humorously introduces the notion of mental radio stations.

Sharon Salzberg. *Lovingkindness: The Revolutionary Art of Happiness*. Boston: Shambhala, 1995. A rich discussion of Buddhist loving-kindness meditation, and of ways to integrate it into daily life.

17. GOD IN DISGUISE

Then the king will say to those on his right hand, "You have my Father's blessing; come, enter and possess the kingdom that has been ready for you since the world was made. For when I was hungry, you gave me food; when thirsty, you gave me drink; when I was a stranger you took me into your home, when naked you clothed me; when I was ill you came to my help, when in prison you visited me." Then the righteous will reply, "Lord, when was it that we saw you hungry and fed you, or thirsty and gave you drink, a stranger and took you home, or naked and clothed you? When did we see you ill or in prison, and come to visit you?" And the king will answer, "I tell you this: anything you did for one of my brothers here, however humble, you did for me."

— Matthew 25:34–40

he above words attributed to Jesus presents an idea common to many religions: When serving others we are really serving God. The Hindu greeting, "namas te," means roughly, "I bow to the God within you." Mother Teresa, caring for the poor and sick, saw only Christ in a series of guises. A spark of the divine resides in everyone. If we focus on our flawed humanity that's all we'll ever see. But look beneath your neighbor's stained and tattered dress: You may find God in disguise.

Today, approach others as if this were the case. With those you meet, or selected people, imagine that their true self is divine. Shape this game in accord with your own wishes and beliefs. That is, you might choose to see others as Christ; or as angelic messengers, like those to whom Abraham offered hospitality; or as secret Bodhisattvas. Admittedly, the disguises worn can seem quite convincing. You may encounter a surly waitress, a rambunctious child, or a drunk staggering down the street. Don't be taken in. As the spiritual teacher Ram Dass says, they're all "just God in drag."

Behave toward others accordingly. Perhaps you've invited a guest for lunch who's overstayed her welcome. Think again. You'd hardly toss a divine emissary out on her ear. Her visit is an honor and privilege; treat her with corresponding care.

97

Use this idea particularly with those you might overlook or dismiss. It's not so hard to see God in your best friend at a party, but what of the young man, lacking in interpersonal skills, sitting all alone in the corner? Include him in the conversation. What of the party show-off who seems a bit of a buffoon? Look beneath the surface. Welcome him into your heart.

It can also be helpful, if challenging, to work specifically with the categories mentioned in the Matthew quote. For example, is there a way through actions or prayer that you could reach out today to those hungry, estranged, ill, or imprisoned? These categories can be understood metaphorically as well as literally: for example, you might have a friend "imprisoned" by alcoholism, or someone you've made a "stranger" by casting them out of your heart. They, too, are God in disguise.

So, at work, are the secretary and the boss, the mail clerk and the CEO. This game obliterates such distinctions. As you circulate through the office, be helpful and respectful to them all.

You might also choose to focus on a person you're intimate with, like a relative, roommate, or partner. You know their human failings all too well. Today focus instead on their divinity, and you may be surprised by what you see.

Helpful Hints

See the God by seeing the good. One way to see the divine in people is to insist on noticing their virtues. Sure they have flaws that drive you up the wall; selfishness, affectations, and annoying habits galore. Guess what? You do, too. But there is goodness at your core and this is no less true of others. And the more you focus on their Godlike attributes, the more you help them live up to this higher self.

Of course, you shouldn't tolerate any abusive behavior. If needed, you can remind the other that he or she is better than that. Help them see their own divine potential.

We're all divinely different. Treating those you meet as *God-like* need not mean you treat them all *alike.* As a rainbow of colors results when white light is diffracted, so individuals express Spirit in unique ways. God is there in your daughter's sense of humor, your colleague's keen intelligence, your grandfather's caring heart. You, in turn, have unique relations with each of these people. Don't stamp your responses with an unchanging mold. Delight in the diversity.

A little at a time is a good place to start. If you try to view everyone as God all at once, you might feel overwhelmed and give up. Better to begin a bit at a time. Taking the train? See the God in that harried man selling you the ticket. Offer him a smile and kind word. Be thoughtful with the woman sitting next to you. Don't battle so hard for the armrest.

Over time these small gestures can sink into your heart and affect many other encounters.

99

Related Readings

Mother Teresa. *In My Own Words*. Liguori, MO: Liguori, 1996. She describes here and elsewhere her vision of Christ in the poor and suffering to whom she ministered.

Alan Watts. *The Book: On the Taboo Against Knowing Who You Are*. New York: Vintage Books, 1966. Influenced by Eastern religions, Watts encourages us to look beyond the small self we think we are, to discover our true divinity.

18. GIVE, GIVE, Give

One day a man asked a sheikh how to reach God. "The ways to God," the sheikh replied, "are as many as there are created beings. But the shortest and easiest is to serve others, not to bother others, and to make others happy."

—Abu Sai'id, in *Essential Sufism,* ed. James Fadiman
and Robert Frager

this is a simple game: just give, give, give. Simple, but not always easy. All too often we view the world through "I-glasses." "What will *I* get out of this situation in terms of profit, pleasure, power, or prestige?" Today, reverse that focus. Ask instead, "What can I give to *others*?"

Remember that some of the best gifts come in small packages. Driving to work, you let someone merge in ahead of your car. His day, and yours, is off to a better beginning. Stopping for coffee you pick up extra donuts for your co-workers. Hey, this could start a trend. Who knows—you might even end up liking each other.

Make a game of noticing what you can't see when wearing I-glasses: the opportunities for service that surround you. A colleague looks dour. Tell her some joke you heard. It just might bring a smile. Open the door for that poor parent struggling with a baby stroller. Give a call to your friend whose mother is seriously ill. Can't reach her? You can always say a prayer for them both, that they be granted strength and healing. And while doing this you can even empty the dishwasher *though it isn't exactly your turn.*

At the same time, don't forget to give to yourself. Depleted and resentful, you'd be of little use to anyone. So give yourself the rest, pleasure, and encouragement you need in order to keep giving to others.

It can be fun to keep a running list of the ways you give, and learn from it about yourself. Which kinds of service seemed to come most naturally? Which gave you the most satisfaction? These might reflect your own gifts, be it a sense of humor, a compassionate heart, or particular skills like baking or organizing. Such talents, properly used, may prove the means of your greatest service.

Notice, too, when it is hard to give. What got in the way? Don't condemn yourself, but simply observe. Often this is the first step toward overcoming these limits. If you play the game again and again, you might challenge yourself (or pray for help) to give a little more in these difficult areas.

But don't demand to be perfect by next Tuesday. Remember that one of the best things you can do is to *give* yourself a break.

Helpful Hints

"Give" is a many splendored word. Different uses of the word can suggest forms of service you might not otherwise consider. Starting to criticize someone in your head? Give them the benefit of the doubt. Jealous of another's success? Give credit where credit is due. Talking with a friend? Give them your full attention. Angry at a perceived slight? For-give and forget.

When possible, give quietly. It's tempting to do service in ways that draw attention to yourself. After all, we want to feel good, have people realize our nobility, and reward us with gratitude and praise. But when they don't we may grow resentful. Our giving was undermined by self-serving motives.

Today, as much as possible, be content to give in quiet ways. Perhaps you clean the carpet and no one notices. The temptation is to shout it from the rooftops: "Look, oh spouse, see what I have wrought!" *Give* it a rest. Remind yourself it's actually better (ouch) if no one's making a fuss. You're trying to learn to give for its own sake. With this in mind, you can admire the clean carpet, and give yourself a pat on the back.

Give to God. In many spiritual paths, service to others is also seen as service to God. After all, the Divine dwells within everyone (see #17 "God in Disguise").

This thought can add another dimension to the game. You praise Granny Emma's prune whip surprise, clear the table, then give Uncle Ed a ride home. Imagine you're doing this all for God. Then the need for others' recognition and thanks diminishes. After all, you're just giving back a small part of the rich life that God has given to you.

Related Readings

103

Ram Dass and Paul Gorman. *How Can I Help?: Stories and Reflections on Service.* New York: Alfred A. Knopf, 1985. A marvelous discussion of the personal and spiritual joys of service, and of the many hazards (self-righteousness, detachment, fear, burnout) that can undermine our giving.

Eknath Easwaran. *Gandhi the Man: The Story of His Transformation.* Petaluma, CA: Nilgiri Press, 1978. See this or other biographies for an account of Gandhi's practice of karma yoga: the spiritual path of selfless service. (Along these lines, see books by and about Mother Teresa, the Dalai Lama, and other notable givers.)

19. LEGGO and LET GOD

Petitionary prayer need not be confined to our own needs.
It may focus on the needs of other persons or situations; then it is
usually called intercessory prayer . . . even at the most individual and
most free and responsible pinnacle of our being, we are open to being
helped and brothered by other souls.
Intercession is the most intensely social act of which the human
being is capable. When carried on secretly, it is mercifully preserved
from, in fact, almost immunized against, the possible corruptions to
which all outer deeds of service for others are subject.

—Douglas V. Steere, *Dimensions of Prayer*

In today's game, focus on giving to others not so much through overt acts, as through prayers for their well-being. This can be done at specific times set aside in the morning or evening, and/or woven throughout your day.

If you wish, let your prayers take the form of petitions to a personal God voiced in words that feel natural to you. But if you're agnostic, uncomfortable with "prayer" per se, don't turn to another game yet. You can still play this in your own way. Simply send out to the universe thoughts of compassion and goodwill (see #16 "WLUV") for the people referred to in this game.

And who are the people for whom you are to pray? Include at least one person or group from each of five categories: Let LEGGO be your mnemonic.

L stands for *loved ones*. Choose one or more loved ones, such as friends or family members. Don't simply mutter a formulaic prayer on their behalf. Spend a little time thinking of their needs, raising these up to Spirit, asking for the help that would be most beneficial. As much as possible, let prayer flow spontaneously from the heart. Be honest, not phoney. Yet be sure your focus is not on changes *you* would like ("Dear Lord, please improve my sister Moira's disposition!"), but on what would truly make the other happy.

E stands for *enemies*. The Biblical injunction to "pray for your enemies" may be applied to anyone with whom you experience conflict. (Some loved ones may reappear in this category.) Perhaps a housemate hogs the bathroom, causing a passing annoyance. Or a long-standing grievance comes to mind: "I brought the car to that mechanic six months ago and it still isn't fixed right!" Bring one or more such "enemies" into prayer. Reverse the energy of your anger into prayers for their well-being. What at first seems a hollow exercise can in time bring about a genuine change of heart. (If you feel blocked here, see #9 "Unpointing the Finger," or other games of acceptance and forgiveness.)

The first *G* in LEGGO stands for those in special need of *gifts, graces, and guidance.* You may know people struggling with illness, financial problems, emotional difficulties, personal losses, or hard decisions. Choose one or more such persons as a prayer-focus in this category. Send them thoughts of good will. Ask that the universe supply them with the strength or help they need to deal successfully with their challenges.

106

And that's not all. The second *G* stands for a *group* that could also use prayer. You may feel special compassion for certain kinds of people on the basis of your life experience. Perhaps you were once laid off at work, and remember well the pain. Pray for all those unable to find a job. Or maybe the morning newspaper jolts you with morbid headlines. You read of victims of domestic abuse, prisoners on death row, children growing up in time of war. It's a lot to digest with your cereal. The temptation is to shut down, or run for the funnies. But first say a prayer on behalf of whichever group has touched your heart.

The last letter *O* of our prayer-fest stands for *ourselves.* During the day situations arise with which you too could use greater-than-human help. Ask God or the universe for the strength, clarity, or specific assistance you need to best deal with your problems. In line with today's game, your spirit in doing so should not be exclusively self-serving. Rather, you are seeking to become whole in a way that will also benefit others.

Children play with LEGOs (construction blocks), building towers out of interlocking pieces. In this LEGGO game, you build an edifice of prayer. Then LEGGO (let go) and let God do His or Her thing. Give your requests over to the universe, trusting in a Higher Power.

To prevent the LEGGO pieces from getting all mixed up, you may wish to keep a written record. Divide a piece of paper into five boxes or columns, one for each category of prayer. You can write in the names of those you are praying for and the requests you have made.

It can be interesting to review such a list sometime later and note prayers which seem to have been answered. Remember, though, answers may come in a different form than you anticipated. "God's ways are not our own."

If you play this game more than once, you might add new people each time to your list, or persist with your original prayer-focus. You might also choose one person a day whom you will pray for at length. It can help to set a time goal such as five minutes, ten, or even a half-hour, to pray just for one individual. It's a stretch, but such concentrated prayer can release surprising wellsprings of insight and compassion.

Helpful Hints

Weave prayer into the tapestry of your day. You might commit to specific times to play the LEGGO game. First-thing-in-the-morning prayer gets the day off to a good start before we're swept away by demands. It can also help to do a LEGGO session when getting ready for bed. Loving thoughts prepare the mind for a restful sleep.

But also make prayer an ongoing part of the day. Perhaps driving to work you automatically switch the radio on to blasting music, news reports, and ads. Today, reserve a few minutes for prayer. And, what if while driving someone cuts you off in traffic? You ordinarily let loose with a volley of curses. Today, see it as a chance to pray for a new-found "enemy" you can convert into a friend. "Dear God, that guy is driving nutso. Please protect him and others on the road. And please help him with whatever problem is making him drive like that."

In such ways, your day will provide a constant stream of opportunities to pray for loved ones, enemies, and those in need, including (most certainly) yourself.

Act on your prayers. Prayer is a two-way street. As you send requests toward the Divine, you may sense some of them rebounding in your own direction. You realize ways you, yourself, could help someone in distress, or be a little more loving with a "loved one." Keep a pen and paper handy to write down prayer-generated ideas. Whenever possible, act on them. You may or may not believe prayer changes outward conditions directly. But it surely changes your heart and helps you make a difference.

Related Readings

Larry Dossey. *Healing Words: The Power of Prayer and the Practice of Medicine.* New York: HarperCollins, 1993. A physician's review of the scientific evidence suggesting that intercessory prayer and "distant healing" have very real effects.

Douglas V. Steere. *Dimensions of Prayer: Cultivating a Relationship with God.* Nashville: Upper Room Books, 1962. A searching exploration of prayer, its meaning and techniques, and its relationship to action.

20. GOLDEN-RULING

What is hateful to you, do not to your fellow man.
That is the entire Law; all the rest is commentary.
—The Talmud, The Shabat (Jewish) 31A

Always treat others as you would like them to treat you:
That is the Law and the prophets.
—New Testament (Christian), Matthew 7:12

Do naught unto others which would cause you pain if done to you.
—The Mahabharata (Hindu) 5:1517

Hurt not others in ways that you yourself would find hurtful.
—The Udana-Varga (Buddhist) 5:18

Never do to others what you would not like them to do to you.
—The Analects of Confucius (Confucian) 15:23

a cross divergent cultures and historical periods one notion surfaces time and again. It's been nicknamed the golden rule—treat others as you would have them treat you. This rule has a psychological dimension: Through awareness of our own wants we better understand those of others. It also has a moral dimension: Fairness involves equal treatment for all. Our own wishes don't justify stomping on others, no matter how tempting this may be. Most importantly, the rule has a spiritual dimension. In treating others like ourselves, we experience a deeper connection with them. We realize a Spirit that unites us all and is expressed through loving concern.

Of course, being told to follow a rule can be a turnoff. But a game, to be fun and interesting, has to have rules. Today, play the game of life with a focus on the golden rule. Take your own wishes, even your own sense of self, and flip it around to help awaken you to others.

You might begin with a person you ordinarily disregard. The postman drops off the mail in the morning—you rarely give it a second thought. Today, do. This person is more than some minor character who briefly appears onstage in the play about your life. He actually has a life of his own! Ask yourself, "If I were that postman how would I want to be treated?" Maybe you'd wish for a kind greeting. A moment of friendly conversation to liven the tedious route, but not too much since there's mail to be delivered.

This way of golden-ruling starts with the other. You imagine yourself into their position and respond to their needs. However, another strategy is to begin with yourself. All day long you experience desires welling up from within. You can pursue them in a self-centered way. But, today, flip them around to become more considerate of those around you.

Say you stumble in the door after a hard day at work. You want your partner to listen to your battle stories and tend to your wounds with the patience of a Florence Nightingale. Flip it around and golden-rule it. He or she might want the same thing too. "How was your day?" you ask, hard as it is to force the words out. "Can I fix you a cup of tea? Or something stiffer?" If you'd appreciate this loving treatment, it's a good bet your partner will as well.

Who's the winner? The other person's clearly better off. So are you, as your insight and compassion grow. Tension in the relationship ("No, it's *my* turn to bitch first!") gives way to a bit more harmony. That's what's so golden about this rule. Somehow, it makes everyone a winner.

In applying this game, you can challenge yourself in a number of ways. For example, you might set a goal for how many people you'd like to golden-rule during the day: three, five, seven? Then, too, you might choose to focus your efforts on someone with whom you're at odds. See their side. Treat them with the same care and respect with which you'd like to be treated.

You might also golden-rule at least one person whose life seems extremely different from your own. What's it like to be that street person? That elderly man serving you coffee, your surly teenager, or that co-worker of a different race or gender? So often we see only what sets us apart. Use the golden rule: It helps link us together.

Helpful Hints

Adjust for personal differences. Treating others as you'd wish to be treated doesn't mean everyone's the same. Maybe after a hard day you want to talk it through, but what if your partner's more of an introvert? Perhaps the most restorative thing, from his or her perspective, is to be left alone to unwind. Adjust for these differences. It's not a violation of the golden rule but a more subtle way to apply it. After all, you'd want others to be sensitive to your individuality. Do the same for them.

113

Don't demand instant reciprocation. In golden-ruling others, a wish—or possibly a demand—may arise that they return the favor. And this should be just at the time and in the form you specify. "When the baby started to cry, I let you sleep last night. Tonight I'm exhausted. Where's my payback?!"

Give-and-take contracts can be valid, but they're hardly the point of this game. You're golden-ruling for its own sake. Others may well reciprocate, but you set yourself up for resentment and disappointment if you demand this be the case. The golden rule quickly turns to brass.

User's warning: Don't lose or abuse yourself. There's a hazard, for
some, to this game. You might be the sort to focus too much on
what other people are feeling and wanting, without proper concern for yourself. This game can seem an invitation to go further
in that direction. Always "doing for others," you could end up
feeling used or abused.

But remember that the golden rule begins with healthy self-
regard. In order to treat others as you'd wish to be treated, you
must be aware of and respect your own desires.

If this is a problem for you, turn the golden rule around. That is,
treat yourself as you might another person. Give yourself the same
love, attention, and care that you would offer a neighbor in need.

114

Related Readings

Ram Dass and Mirabai Bush. *Compassion in Action: Setting Out on the
Path of Service.* New York: Bell Tower, 1992. A personal and practical
guide for how to integrate service more deeply into one's life.

Matthew Fox. *A Spirituality Named Compassion and the Healing of the
Global Village, Humpty Dumpty and Us.* San Francisco:
HarperSanFrancisco, 1979. A meditation, by an unorthodox priest, on
the personal and global significance of compassion—that ability to
enter into another's experience.

Part Five
CONTACTING the
DIVINE

the games up to this point have kept us busy. We've been celebrating, accepting, forgiving, loving, serving, generating positive habits of the heart. But we can travel only so far under our own steam. Mystics across the world agree: To truly transform we need divine assistance. "Unless the Lord builds the house, those who build it labor in vain" (Psalm 127:1). Previous games may have mentioned a Higher Power, or left that notion implicit. Now we place it front and center. We're seeking nothing less than contact with the Divine.

Of course, this Power goes by many titles. We may call it God, Allah, the Tao, Christ, the Great Mother, Buddha, Nature, or any other name. We can conceive of it as a Person to whom we pray, the true Self within, or a Force underlying all things. People the world over seem to tap into the same transcendent source despite their distinct approaches. Nor would it be better to get rid of these differences. In the words of Hindu teacher Prema Chaitanya in *Vedanta and the West*, "How artistic that there should be room for such variety—how rich the texture is, and how much more interesting than if the Almighty had decreed one antiseptically safe, exclusive, orthodox way. Although he is Unity, God finds, it seems, his recreation in variety!"

The games I supply for contacting the Divine are varied. They draw on our different powers: reading, writing, talking, visualizing, and prayer. What works best for one person may do nothing for another; you need to choose the style that suits you, or seek spiritual guidance on the matter. You should also recognize that your methods may shift over time, as your intuition leads you creatively forward.

If these games differ in form, they also allow you to fill in the content according to your own beliefs. The mantra used in "Plugging In"; the spiritual passage read for "Lectio Divina"; the content of the "God Letters" you write: These are entirely up to you. Nothing could be more personal than our communications with the Divine. Yet in their personal nature resides their power. God appears not as some distant ideal, some matter for theological debate, but as a personal source of strength, insight, and love that alters one's life for the better.

That's not to say results are always immediate. In the words of the Native American shaman, Black Elk, in *The Sacred Pipe*, "It may be that we shall receive no vision or message from the Great Spirit the first time that we 'lament,' yet we may try many times, for we should remember that *Wakan-Tanka* is always anxious to aid those who seek Him with a pure heart." In New Testament terms, we are told to keep knocking and knocking—God will surely open the door.

These, then, are knocking-on-the-door games. The excitement begins as that door cracks open and we catch a glimpse of what lies inside.

21. The (Not So) Imaginary Friend

God does not ask much of us. But remembering Him, asking for His grace, offering Him your troubles, or thanking Him for what He has given you will console you all the time. During your meals or during any daily duty, lift your heart up to Him, because even the least little remembrance will please Him. You don't have to pray out loud; He's nearer than you can imagine.

It isn't necessary that we stay in church in order to remain in God's presence. We can make our heart a chapel where we can go anytime to talk to God privately. These conversations can be so loving and gentle, and anyone can have them. So why not begin?

—Brother Lawrence, *The Practice of the Presence of God*

W

hen you were young you may have had an imaginary friend. Such a companion provides many a child with solace and joy. Yet as we age, we lose our belief in such buddies; we accept that we're largely alone.

But what if the child intuits something the adult forgets? What if we can recover that sense of a friend with us always, providing love and guidance? We may find, with Brother Lawrence, that this simple key can unlock profound treasures of the Spirit.

Today, use your imagination to explore that possibility. All day long, or as often as you remember, hold a running conversation in your head (or out loud) with an imagined Friend.

You might think of this Friend as the God of your understanding. Or you might visualize an enlightened sage—Buddha, a Native American shaman—whatever image works for you. This is a being who possesses the wisdom of the heavens but is delightfully down to earth. She or he is there to laugh with you, celebrate successes, console you in hard times, give direction when you're confused—all the help a best friend might provide.

Now chatter away with abandon. As you go through the day, keep sharing all that happens with your newfound companion. Don't decide that things are too small, or boring, or embarrassing to share. That voice is you talking, not your Friend.

Let loose. For example, "I hate getting stuck at a red light. I know I'm too impatient, but that's how I am. I better not be late . . . you know this is an important meeting. I want to make a good impression. Help! I'm nervous. What should I say when I get there?" Imagine this being knows you well and is lovingly (not judgmentally) concerned with your welfare. She or he can supply the power and guidance you need. So amidst all your talk, also listen for answers. Expect them to come, often through a quiet voice within.

For the fun of it, you might set some goals for yourself. Can you remember to check in with your divine Friend at least once an hour, or more? And how long can you keep the conversation going before you become distracted? Then, too, can you remember to reach out for assistance when you begin to "lose it"—lapse into anger or fear? That's when you most need a friend.

You can also adapt this game to fit your own rhythms. Perhaps you'd like to converse with your Friend first thing upon awakening to help set the day's agenda. Lunchtime can be a good time to walk and talk. Or maybe your Friend is the last person you wish to be with before drifting off to sleep. It's through such small moments and intimacies that the friendship will gradually build.

Helpful Hints

Be patient with yourself. Perhaps you start the day sharing your thoughts and feelings with a spiritual Companion. Then the morning crests into a tidal wave and sweeps you away like a piece of driftwood. Minutes, then hours go by before you realize you left your Friend home with the breakfast dishes.

Don't feel a failure. Habits are hard to break. You're probably used to operating on automatic or, when you need to process events, relying on the mind's inner monologue. Now you're learning a radically new habit: that of dialoguing with the Divine. It may not come easily. But your focus strengthens with repetition just like muscles exerted against weights.

Be honest. In this conversation/prayer, you may wish to express holy sentiments, such as "Thy will be done, O Divine Master." Fine if you mean it, but do an honesty check. Maybe it's truer to say, "Hey Goddess (Buddha . . .), I want to get *my will* done. Where do I go from here?" Of course, your spiritual Friend might take you to new places, but only if you're honest about where you are to begin with.

Then, too, you may feel frustrated by talking to a being you can neither see nor hear. Share that, as well, in conversation: "Hey, God, how do I know you're there? I feel like I'm jabbering into a void." Maybe you'll get an immediate answer. Even if not, your very persistence in questioning may pull you closer to Spirit.

Related Readings

Sue Monk Kidd. *God's Joyful Surprise: Finding Yourself Loved*. San Francisco: HarperSanFrancisco, 1987. The moving story of the author's transition from a duty-driven, stress-filled brand of religion, to one based on a personal relation with God.

Frank Laubach. *Laubach's Prayer Diary*. Westwood, NJ: Fleming H. Revell, 1964. The diaries of a priest who sets for himself a grand experiment: to try to remain with God each waking moment. A vivid recounting of his struggles and, more so, his joys.

Brother Lawrence. *The Practice of the Presence of God*. Springdale, PA: Whitaker House, 1982. In this simple classic, a seventeenth-century monk describes methods and benefits of conversing with God.

22. The INNER ELDER

As depth psychology reveals, every culture has different archetypal images that serve as access codes to elder wisdom. Often these images take the form of a Wise Old Man or Woman, a personification of the psyche that has panoramic knowledge that is unavailable to normal consciousness. When the elder appears in our dreams as a male figure, he may take the form of a guru, shaman, or magician. . . . When the elder appears as a Wise Old Woman, she may be a priestess, sorceress, earth mother, or goddess. Frequently she appears as the crone, the wise woman past childbearing age honored in prepatriarchal societies for her serenity and spiritual power.

—Zalman Schacter-Shalomi and Ronald S. Miller, *From Age-ing to Sage-ing: A Profound New Vision of Growing Older*

Imagine that within you there is a personal guide and mentor—an inner elder. No matter what your age, this being is older and wiser than you. Long life has given him or her access to precious gifts of the Spirit. Now the elder wishes to use these for your aid.

To contact this being, take a few minutes apart from the world. Find a cozy corner where you will not be disturbed. If you wish, put on some soothing music, light a candle, or use any other device to relax and deepen your awareness.

Now go within and allow an image of your inner elder to surface. What does this person look like? Is it male or female, of a particular race or culture? (It could even be non-human.) Let yourself be surprised. What qualities radiate from his or her face and bearing: wisdom, compassion, or childlike joy? Notice any other details of the elder's dress, activity, or of the background landscape. (If no clear visualization comes, don't worry or give up. You may still sense a kind of presence, or special messages meant for you.)

Now in your mind, begin to speak with the elder. You may have a particular question to ask, or a problem with which you could use some help. Pose the issue. You need not go into great detail; the elder already knows you from the inside out. Even when you were unaware of it this person watched over you with love.

Now listen for the elder's counsel. This may come in the form of words, gestures, or an intuitive feeling welling up from within. He or she may offer a way to resolve your dilemma. Or perhaps you are helped to see it from a new perspective, more expansive than your narrow view.

Leave time for open exchange. Is there anything else you wish to ask, or simply to talk over with this newfound mentor? Conversely, is there any message the elder longs to communicate— something that might help you in life's journey?

When the time seems right, say good-bye in whatever way seems appropriate. Bring the meditation to a close. But know that this inner elder remains ready to aid you whenever you so desire.

During the day, as the need or opportunity arises, take a few minutes to check back in. Again, imagine the elder there with you. Again, raise any question or issue you wish. Sense the loving response and that elder's healing presence.

Helpful Hints

Expect the unusual. Don't presume you know what your inner elder will look like. You may be expecting a wise old man with a beard. Instead you're surprised by an impish crone dressed in outlandish garments. Or perhaps your inner guru is a character straight from a children's movie you saw last week with your kids. That's fine. It doesn't mean the messages you receive will be silly or superficial. That image is unlocking a part of your soul that longs for self-expression.

Allow for change and multiplicity. Your image of the inner elder may shift over time. Perhaps you started with a great aunt of yours whom you associate with good cooking and homey advice. Next time a Native American sage appeared, gazing across the plains. How interesting. Maybe your inner needs have changed. Then, too, you may be meant to work with more than one figure, each offering its own form of help.

Look around you for models. Each of us, and the world in general, is in need of the elder-wisdom valued in traditional societies but largely neglected in our own. Perhaps older mentors have blessed your life. If so, these real people—a loving grandparent, perhaps, or a senior friend or colleague—may appear as the inner elder you visualize. That's fine. This meditation may help awaken you to the wise elders that surround you.

It can also inspire you to seek out such people. Don't hesitate to pose questions to them, as you would to your inner elder. Also, realize you are in training for your own elderhood. This need not be a time of diminishment, but of spiritual growth and fulfillment.

Related Readings

Maria Harris. *Jubilee Time: Celebrating Women, Spirit, and the Advent of Age.* New York: Bantam Books, 1995. Based on biblical teachings concerning the Jubilee (fiftieth) year, a series of illuminating teachings and exercises for women coming of age.

Drew Leder. *Spiritual Passages: Embracing Life's Sacred Journey.* New York: Jeremy P. Tarcher/Putnam, 1997. Through stories drawn from diverse wisdom traditions, I explore ways to age creatively and spiritually in life's second half.

Zalman Schachter-Shalomi and Ronald S. Miller. *From Age-ing to Sage-ing: A Profound New Vision of Growing Older.* New York: Warner Books, 1995. A wonderful book on how to use the aging process as a stimulus to spiritual growth for the healing of self, community, and planet.

23. Plugging in

The mantram is the living symbol of the profoundest
that the human being can conceive of, the highest that we can
respond to and love. When we repeat the mantram in our mind,
we are reminding ourselves of this supreme Reality enshrined in
our hearts. It is only natural that the more we repeat the
mantram, the deeper it will sink into our consciousness. As it
goes deeper, it will strengthen our will, heal the old divisions in
our consciousness that now cause us conflict and turmoil, and
give us access to deeper resources of strength, patience, and love to
work for the benefit of those around us.

—Eknath Easwaran, *A Mantram Handbook*

imagine you're a sort of tape player, flashlight, or other appliance. As long as you're plugged into a power source you can perform your function with excellence and ease. You play songs, shine brightly, or do whatever else you do. But what happens when you're unplugged? If you also have batteries, you'll continue to work for a while. With time, however, your performance will decay. Your music will slow, or your light will dim, and then you'll lose power entirely.

Today, use a time-honored device to remain plugged into a (Higher) Power source. This device is called a mantra: a brief prayer mentally repeated again and again. Almost every religion has its versions. A mantra can be a short formula of praise, such as the Jewish "Barukh attah Adonai" (Blessed are thou, O Lord), or the Islamic "Allahu akbar" (God is great). Some mantras take the form of petitions for help. Variations on the "Jesus prayer"—"Lord Jesus Christ, Son of God, have mercy on me"—have been used for centuries, and are particularly key in Eastern Orthodox practices. The simplest mantra is a divine name. Gandhi died from an assassin's bullet with "Ram," the name of a Hindu deity, on his lips. However, not all mantras invoke a personal God. A Buddhist favorite—"Om mani padme hum"—can be translated as "the jewel in the lotus of the heart," referring to the pure nature within each person. A mantra proclaims, and reconnects us with, our deepest spiritual source.

Today, make repeated use of a mantra. Choose one or more that speaks to your heart. Imagine you are using it to plug into a Higher Power. You don't have to run, and run life, on your own little batteries. You can connect to an unlimited Source. You might pretend that your spiritual connector also has a "groundwire." The mantra will keep you mentally grounded, discharging any negative energies such as anxiety and anger.

Your first question is probably what mantra to use. Some spiritual teachers advocate selecting one, like those above, whose sound, meaning, and power have been tested over the centuries. However, there's also something to be said for making up your own. Relying on prayer or intuition, you may arrive at a mantra that speaks to you personally. This could be an affirmation such as, "I'm a child of God, loved without limit." It might be an assertion of peace, joy, or faith: "All shall be well." The mantra may call you to your better self: "Help me to give, and love, and serve." Or it may remind you to be grateful for what you already have: "Thanks for the blessings that surround me." Feel free to draw on a favorite line of scripture, such as "The Lord is my shepherd, I shall not want" (see #4 "Surfing the Psalm").

Whether you select a time-honored formula or make up your own, you might want to stick with only one mantra. Repeated over days, weeks, even years, it forms a powerful and direct connection with the divine. We might call this the DC (direct current) approach to plugging in.

However, it can also be rewarding to play with a number of mantras, turning to each according to your needs. Call this the AC (alternating current) approach. You might have one mantra for times of agitation: "Peace I grant you, peace throughout the land." When you're slipping into morbid guilt, you call upon another: "God loves me just as I am: a human being who makes mistakes." At times of fear, you use a third: "I rest safe in the arms of my savior." Keep listening for the mantras that will best serve.

But don't wait for crises to get started. It can be helpful to plug into a mantra when you first wake up, or in your morning shower. Simply repeat the chosen phrase inside your mind. You could set a goal for yourself, like saying your mantra one hundred times, or for a certain number of minutes.

Throughout the day, return to the mantra whenever you remember or wish. Use it, for example, when doing the dishes or folding laundry. With it you can transform your most ordinary chores into times of sacred prayer. Lunchtime is also a good time to take a mantra break. In the evening your mantra can help you re-center as you prepare for bed.

One beauty of the mantra is that it's right there with you whenever and wherever you wish. Need energy, calm, guidance, help? Start by plugging in.

Helpful Hints

Prayer, not abracadabra. The power of any mantra depends upon the spirit with which you use it. Simply repeated mechanically it may have little effect. Nor is it a magic formula that compels a genie to appear and fix all of your problems. Rather, it's a way to open you to the Divine. The more you say it in a prayerful and receptive spirit, the more you will sense its power.

Make up playful variations. There are many ways to keep your mantra-play fun and creative. For example, you might write a number of different mantras, each on a separate slip of paper, and place them in a box. In the morning reach in and pull one out. Use whichever you've picked as your mantra for the day; assume the Universe guided your choice.

131

Think it, say it, sing it. There are also many ways to say a mantra. You can repeat it in your mind at whatever pace seems appropriate. (You might time the cadence to your breathing.) You can also chant the mantra mentally using a simple sequence of notes. For that matter, you can say or sing it out loud; try it when taking a walk. A sung mantra also makes a nice lullaby to put you or your child to sleep.

With time, it may seem like the mantra's practically saying itself. You merely sit back and listen.

132

Related Readings

Eknath Easwaran. *Meditation.* Petaluma, CA: Nilgiri Press, 1978. The author presents an eight-point program for living a spiritual life, with a key focus on use of a mantrum.

The Way of a Pilgrim and *The Pilgrim Continues His Way,* trans. R. M. French. San Francisco: HarperSanFrancisco, 1952. These two works by an anonymous nineteenth-century Russian monk wonderfully illustrate the transformative power of a mantra (in this case, the Jesus prayer).

24. LECTIO DIVINA

He entered a village where a woman whose name was Martha welcomed him. She had a sister named Mary who sat beside the Lord at his feet listening to him speak. Martha, burdened with much serving, came to him and said, "Lord, do you not care that my sister has left me by myself to do the serving? Tell her to help me." The Lord said to her in reply, "Martha, Martha, you are anxious and worried about many things. There is need of only one thing. Mary has chosen the better part and it will not be taken from her."

—*Luke 10:38–42*

I n the Middle Ages, monks and nuns would work intimately with Scripture through a method known as *lectio divina*. Translated, that means "divine reading." A passage would be read, savored word by word, contemplated over time, and prayed through, until divine shafts of meaning penetrated the reader's heart like light through a stained-glass window. We might compare the reader to Mary in the parable above. As she sits quietly at a teacher's feet, so the reader does with a text, seeking illumination.

In this modern-day adaptation, begin by choosing a passage to read. It might come from a spiritual source, such as a psalm, Gospel parable, Buddhist tale, or African teaching story. It can also be a "secular" passage which nonetheless has sacred meaning for you—for example, the words of a popular song, or a poem that carries you outward into the splendors of nature or inward to the secrets of the soul.

How to locate your material? You might sit quietly until you arrive at an intuitive idea of the text you are to work with. Perhaps it will be something with which you're already familiar that has resonated over the years. Follow this inner direction. You might scan your bookshelf until the appropriate work leaps out and tweaks your nose. You can also take a book important to you and open it at random, seeing where your gaze first falls. If the passage seems inappropriate, forget it. But you might be surprised to find the words you've opened to speak directly to your condition. Then, too, there are many excellent collections of spiritual writings, stories, prayers, and meditations. You might skim one through until something catches your eye and touches your heart.

Once you have your passage, read through it slowly. Linger over any words or images that seem particularly telling. Imagine that this text is addressing you personally; try to hear the messages conveyed.

For example, if working with the story quoted above, you might place yourself within it. Do you have a Martha-self, bustling from carpool, to office, to grocery store, becoming uncentered from so much activity? Maybe the passage is calling you to be still.

Or do you identify with Mary? Perhaps you recently quit a volunteer job and have a lingering sense of guilt. This passage may confirm your decision and help ease your mind. You've "chosen the better part"—you needed some space in your life. And, by God, "it will not be taken from you."

Maybe the words that leap out are those that juxtapose Martha's "many things," with Mary's "one." Are you dissipating energy on trivia, when there's one thing that should now be your life-focus? And what is that one thing: family; personal healing; a relationship with God?

Feel free to challenge your reading. For example, perhaps Jesus strikes you as just plain insensitive. It's Martha, after all, who's doing all the work. Do you sometimes feel similarly unappreciated? Argue Martha's side. Imagine Jesus' reply.

In such ways interrogate your passage and let it question you back. Rely not only on your intellect, but on a divine Spirit that can help illuminate your reading. For medieval monks and nuns, *lectio divina* wasn't of much use unless touched by the finger of God.

You might do this divine reading in the morning, then keep the passage in mind throughout the day. If possible, let it influence your thought and conduct. For example, the above story might lead you to be a little more Mary-like: taking needed breaks, seeking focus, and spending quiet time with Spirit. Your reading might even suggest larger life changes. Dare to listen and act.

If you play this game more than one day, you might then go on to a new passage. Perhaps your first one set off a train of thought that leads you naturally to your next selection. On the other hand, you might choose to stay a while longer with the original. Like a many-faceted jewel it can reveal new meanings as you rotate it slowly in your heart.

Over time, instead of using a prepackaged daily meditation book, why not compile your own? Simply start a journal where you write down these special passages. Also leave room to record your own reflections on each. In this way, "divine reading" can be enriched by a little "divine writing" in a dialogue of the soul.

Helpful Hints

Convert everyday reading into lectio divina. The technique you're learning here can be applied to any text, any time, when a passage especially strikes you. Don't just rush on to the next page in a feverish race to finish whatever you're reading. Pause to savor those particular words. Explore why they touched you so. The longer you linger the more you open to *lectio divina.*

Memorize. Did you ever have to memorize and recite a passage in class? If this brings back gruesome memories, put them aside. When we do it because we want to, memorization can be a pleasure. We come to know words by heart— that is, they sink inside, become a place we can go when in need of inspiration or solace (see #4 "Surfing the Psalm" and #23 "Plugging In"). So consider memorizing, line by line, the passages that mean the most to you.

Let words lead to acts. In the Gospel passage quoted above, we can imagine Jesus telling Martha, "Don't just do something, sit there!" This is in the spirit of *lectio divina;* we suspend outer activity long enough to absorb a needed teaching. But there comes a time, as well, to put that teaching into effect: Don't just sit there forever—do something! That is, allow your *lectio divina* to make a difference in your day. Whatever changes you make need not be dramatic, or even evident to others. But let your passage transform you somehow. Otherwise, it may become just a bunch of words, quickly receding from relevance and memory.

Related Readings

Christina Feldman and Jack Kornfield. *Soul Food: Stories to Nourish the Spirit and Heart.* San Francisco: HarperSanFrancisco, 1991. These Buddhist teachers have assembled a collection of spiritual tales from diverse traditions, organized by topic and suitable for *lectio divina.*

Richard J. Foster. *Prayer: Finding the Heart's True Home.* New York: HarperCollins, 1992. A thoughtful exploration of twenty-one different forms of prayer in all, including a discussion of *lectio divina.* (See also the collection he edited with James Smith, *Devotional Classics* [HarperSanFrancisco, 1990], for a set of readings in the Christian tradition appropriate for *lectio divina.*)

Marilyn Sewell, ed. *Cries of the Spirit: A Celebration of Women's Spirituality.* Boston: Beacon Press, 1991. An anthology of spiritual writings, suitable for close reading, mainly poetry by and for women.

25. GOD LETTERS

In the faces of men and women I see God,
and in my own face in the glass,
I find letters from God dropt in the street, and every one
is sign'd by God's name,
And I leave them where they are, for I know that wheresoe'er I go,
Others will punctually come for ever and ever.

—Walt Whitman, "Song of Myself," from *Leaves of Grass*

there's something special about a letter. Over the phone, words fly back and forth, and then vanish. Letters, by contrast, linger. We can read them again and again at our leisure. We can write them with care, working out our ideas as we go. Sometimes, nothing's better than an exchange of letters to bring good friends together.

Today, pull away at least once to correspond with a most special friend. And who is this? None other than God. Or, if this notion doesn't work for you, imagine yourself writing to a spiritual being of your choosing, such as Buddha, Mary, or a wise old crone.

Begin by finding a time and place to be quiet. Let your mind calm and center. You are about to write to your Friend. Of course, there are letters and there are *letters*. The first type is newsy and superficial, sent to renew an acquaintance or fulfill a duty. The second type, rarer in these days of phones and faxes, is those letters where you seek to plumb the depths of who you are and what you're going through. It's in this vein that you write to your divine Correspondent. Set down on paper any issue you're wrestling with, any feelings that are difficult, any sorrow or joy you'd wish to share. If you feel blocked in some area, don't hesitate to ask for help. If gratitude bubbles up, include that too.

Don't worry about expressing yourself eloquently. No other person will see and judge your letter. Nor does it have to be long. Your heart may speak forth in half-formed thoughts and terse phrases. But you might also find that in the flow of a longer letter, feelings and issues crystallize that had previously been unclear.

When your letter is done, pause. Know that it has been instantaneously sent and received by a kind of divine e-mail. A return answer is already on the way. It will come not via the post office or a computer modem, but channeled through your intuitive mind.

When ready, pick up your pen or return to your keyboard. Start writing a second letter. This one begins not "Dear God," but "Dear (your own name)." Your Friend is writing back. Know that what flows forth will be a message of love. It may also embody a playfulness or wisdom beyond that of your unaided mind.

Listen quietly to hear a response within. Let whatever comes come. Set it to paper, word by word, sentence by sentence. Don't try to predict or control this flow of thought. Where's it going next? You'll know when you get there. Also, don't be disturbed if at points the letter seems fragmented or confused. Not every word will be a perfect gem. Your own mind-static may impede transmission. When you sense you have come to the end of the message, sign it "Love, God" (or whatever your Friend's name is), and take a few minutes to ponder its contents. Does the letter provide a message of hope or consolation? Have you received valuable guidance, or a new angle on a problem? There may be some dross to sift out, but pan for any gold.

You might write your letters in a special journal. View them as a precious resource. Re-reading them from time to time can call you back to your center, and stimulate you to further correspondence. This you can undertake when questions or problems arise, or simply as an ongoing practice. Cultivate that new Pen Pal.

Helpful Hints

Set aside the time. It takes a certain amount of time and concentration to sit down and write a letter. For this reason, you might choose to write and receive letters early in the morning before things get too frenzied. The evening, when calm (hopefully) returns, can be a good time to correspond again. But beware of waiting for the "perfect" time—it may never come. (Remember all those letters to friends you never got around to writing?) Set aside whatever time you can.

Use writing as conversation. When you receive back a letter from your spiritual Friend it may raise as many questions as it answers. "What do you mean here?" Or, "How would I act on that piece of advice?" You can pose these queries in a brief follow-up letter, along with anything else you feel moved to say. Then listen for your Friend's reply to your reply, and so on. In this way use letter-writing to initiate a dialogue.

As needed, use shorthand. Especially as you get more used to the game, you may find you and your Friend corresponding in a sort of shorthand. The day is spinning out of control and there's little time for lengthy letters. Stop. Pen a brief note, and jot down any reply you hear. Sometimes a few words can speak volumes.

Ship Higher Power packages. In addition to writing letters, you might also ship packages to your Correspondent. When an issue comes along you don't want to deal with alone—a problem, dilemma, or source of fear—picture yourself packaging it up in a box or brown paper wrapper. Then imagine sending the package to your Higher Power by heavenly express. "There, you take it. It's too much for me." Feel the burden lift. Know the problem rests in stronger hands. If helpful, you might imagine a letter back acknowledging receipt or giving further instructions.

143

Related Readings

A. J. Russell, ed. *God Calling.* New York: Jove Books, 1978. An inspiring collection of the personal messages received by two women joined in prayer some fifty years ago.

Neale Donald Walsch. *Conversations with God: An Uncommon Dialogue, Book 1.* New York: G. P. Putnam and Sons, 1995. The author records the clear and detailed communications he experienced receiving from God.

Part Six

CLAIMING INNER
FREEDOM

t he previous section consisted of games for contacting the Divine. Yet there's a precondition for success with such games, as with all others in this book. We might call it "inner freedom." We need enough space within to gather and focus our mental energies. We then need the freedom to choose where these energies will be directed, and to effectively implement our plan. In the *Gospel of Sri Ramakrishna,* this nineteenth-century Hindu master put it thusly: "No matter what path you follow, yoga [a spiritual discipline] is impossible unless the mind becomes quiet. The mind of a yogi is under his control; he is not under the control of his mind."

But how many of us can consistently claim this mastery? We are pulled apart by a thousand distractions. To use a Hindu analogy, the mind leaps this way and that like a deranged monkey. A few minutes of introspection will often make this clear. "I'm tired of working. I want some chocolate. No, I'll get too fat. I should exercise more. But I don't have the time. How am I ever going to get that mailing done next week? My boss will chew me out if I don't. He has bad breath. Does my breath smell bad, too? . . ." On and on the crazed simian cavorts.

This would be well and good if we simply enjoyed the show. But the truth is it causes us no end of suffering. We may feel haunted by anxiety, driven by anger, trapped by self-hate. We cannot be fully present to the here and now, nor build our connection to the Divine. There's simply too much distraction.

What to do? Thankfully, we can draw on the world's spiritual traditions to help us tame the monkey. Many of these games are based on time-honored practices, albeit given a playful twist. Cultivating the witness; attending to the breath; breaking the hold of self, and of negative thoughts: Each is a way of reclaiming inner freedom. Don't let some monkey lock you in a cage.

26. The WITNESS PROTECTION PROGRAM

The witness is a natural aspect of our minds. It is what the mind does when it is at peace. . . . We are often tormented by agitation, restlessness, fear, doubt, and other disturbing states of mind that cover up the witness. We can rediscover the witness by choosing to look deeply and investigate the process of mind. If we have the patience to watch long enough, we see that the disturbing states of mind come and go. We don't have to base our decisions or actions upon them. We don't have to repress or express them. If we truly see the nature of these mind states—their impersonal, constantly changing quality—our identification with them shatters.

—Diane Mariechild, *Open Mind: Daily Meditations for Becoming Mindful*

Ordinarily, we identify closely with the thoughts that circulate through our mind. This grants them tremendous power. We are tormented by a fear; driven by a desire; trapped in the box of a narrow judgment. For the moment that is *who we are*.

A way out is suggested by Buddhist *Vipassana* (insight) meditation. Teaching a style of detached mindfulness, this ancient practice serves as an inspiration for this game.

Throughout the day watch your mind, as if from outside, simply doing its thing. You might begin with a meditation lasting a few minutes in the morning. Witness your passing thoughts—cravings, sensations, worries, daydreams, random snatches of song. No attic could be as cluttered as our minds; no river so constantly shifting. You might label what your mind is doing at any moment: "Worrying, worrying. Remembering, remembering. Wanting to go to the bathroom." Or simply observe these thoughts come and go.

Throughout the day, as much as possible, reclaim this stance of neutral observer. Do this especially when you can use some detachment from whatever's going on in your head.

Perhaps you're hurrying to prepare for an appointment when you remember to call on the witness. "Anxious," the witness comments. "Rushing, rushing." You pause to scratch an annoying itch. "Scratching." You take some deep breaths and think about your upcoming meeting. "Planning," the witness notes. Though part of you is still trapped in the unfolding drama, part of you, like the audience of a movie, simply sits back and observes.

One thing the witness does not do is to make judgments. From this detached perspective, "anxious" is no better or worse than "calm." They are simply two transitory mental states, one following upon the other. "Planning" is neither bad nor good. It's simply what your mind is doing.

Of course, the mind may judge itself. (In fact, it's something of a judgment machine.) "I can't believe I'm so anxious about this stupid appointment. You'd think I'd be more mature." But the witness doesn't take sides. If such thoughts arise, just observe them like any others: "Judging. Self-hating." More mind-chatter passing through.

Nor does the witness ever seek to intervene and fix matters inside your brain. For example, it does not say, "Stop hating yourself." Yet the witness-stance, by its very nature, facilitates change. Observed from a detached perspective, our thoughts lose some of their compulsive hold and toxicity. As soon as we notice: "Self-hate . . . how interesting," self-hate no longer holds us hostage. We simply watch it arise, crest, and then depart, giving way in time to new feelings. We're safely sheltered in a witness protection program.

If you like keeping score, each time you reenter witness mode you might award yourself a point. Of course, in line with the game, there's no winning or losing. Simply notice how many points you're accumulating; don't judge this as good or bad. Or if you do, just witness that you're judging.

You might also note the situations when it is hardest to invoke the witness—times of fear, perhaps, or anger, or stress. See if you can protect the witness even in the midst of such turmoil. The witness then, in turn, will protect you.

Helpful Hints

This game is cumulative. You may feel beneficial effects at once from playing. However, much of this game's force is established over time. After a few days of repeated witnessing you may feel like someone who, having climbed a hill, has gained a more comprehensive vision of a river in which they'd recently been swimming. You can see the twists and turns of your mental life: how pleasures and sorrows come and go; how frustrations arise and then are resolved. In this swirling river of thought nothing abides except change itself. This perspective can prove a relief, especially when life threatens to suck you under.

Use imagery. In taking on the detached stance of the witness it may help to use mental imagery. Illustrated above is one example: that of seeing your mind as a river of thoughts you are observing from a safe distance. Alternatively, you can visualize your thoughts as so many clouds passing overhead, then disappearing from view. They never permanently mar the clear sky that lies beyond—an image of the true Self.

Or more down to earth, visualize yourself as a spectator at a movie theater. Your life and mind itself is the movie, complete with heroes and villains, shifts of plot, moments of joy and terror. The film can become quite upsetting if you believe it's ultimately real. The fun kicks in when you remember it's just a movie. Sit back and have some popcorn.

Don't forget to breathe. Amidst the storm of your thoughts (to use yet another metaphor) you might like a safe port in which to anchor. Try turning your attention to your breath. Simply watching your breath go in and out can help you calm and recenter. And that leads directly into the next game.

Related Readings

Joseph Goldstein. *The Experience of Insight: A Simple and Direct Guide to Buddhist Meditation.* Boston: Shambhala, 1987. Just what the title states, including a discussion of witness practice.

Jon Kabat-Zinn. *Wherever You Go, There You Are: Mindfulness Meditation in Everyday Life.* New York: Hyperion, 1994. An accessible guide to cultivating awareness of the moment, and of our mental processes.

27. BREATHING
ABCs

*[Breath] connects the human being with the outside
world and the outside world with his inner world. . . . Experiencing the
breath means to start to live in a new way. Breathing became my
"guide rope" that enables me to lead the body and with it the spiritual
and mental into a new "opening" to life.*

—Ilsa Middendorf, *The Perceptible Breath*

s yoga masters have known for centuries, proper breathing is key to freeing up body, mind, and spirit. This is a lesson we need to relearn. In modern Western rush-rush culture, many of us breathe accordingly—quick, shallow breaths. The result is an equally shallow attention-span and a gradual buildup of stress. When we breathe instead with depth and attention, our calmness grows. Our focus strengthens. We're more present to the inner and outer world, and potentially to the divine. In fact, the very word "spirit" comes from the Latin root for "breath."

This game introduces three simple techniques to help breathe more deeply of life. Just call them the Breathing ABCs.

In our ABC, *A* stands for *attention*. Begin by spending a couple of minutes simply attending to your breath. Feel the soft current of air entering your mouth or nostrils. Experience your chest or abdomen expand as you inhale, and then relax on the outbreath. As your mind begins to wander—which it certainly will—simply refocus, when you remember, back to your breathing. It can help to count your breath from one to ten and over again, or to mentally say "rise" with each inhalation, and "fall" as you exhale.

While doing this, don't judge your breathing patterns good or bad (such as "I'm breathing too fast!"). Don't try in any way to alter your breath. Nonetheless, simply from attending to it, your breathing may calm and deepen. You may also find yourself growing more centered in the present moment as you keep your focus on the breath.

B stands for *belly-breathing*. In the second part of this game, breathe from your belly (or to use the formal term, your abdomen). Often we lead with the intercostal muscles of the chest. This produces shorter, shallower breaths. For a sample, place your hands on your chest and pant like a dog—don't worry, nobody's watching. Feel your ribs rise and fall. Now, instead, place your hands on your belly, and allow it to expand on a deep, slow inhalation. (This switchover can be helped along by breathing in through your nose.) Let the air out slowly as the abdomen naturally contracts. Instead of leading with your chest, you're now using your diaphragm to breathe. This helps trigger a relaxation response. Soon you may feel your shoulders drop and your feet tingle with enhanced blood flow. For a couple of minutes simply enjoy belly-breathing. It's like taking off a pair of tight shoes.

C stands for *cleansing*. In this part of the game, use breath-imagery to help cleanse the body and mind. Imagine that each time you inhale, you are breathing in a luminescent golden light. This light has the power to rejuvenate you when tired; soothe jangled nerves; and stimulate positive emotions. Visualize it entering with the breath, then coursing up to your head and outward through the limbs. Everything the light touches it heals.

With each exhalation, imagine you are ridding yourself of any physical or mental toxins. Anxiety? Breathe it out. Anger? Let it go. Muscle tension? Release it each time you exhale. This clears out more space to be filled up by the gold light you're breathing in.

Now you've spent a few minutes practicing your ABCs—Attention, Belly-breathing, Cleansing. Choose one or more method that feels right for you. Continue to use it throughout the day whenever you wish. Simply pause in the middle of work—or shopping, or cooking dinner— to breathe consciously, using one of these techniques. It may also help to set focused goals. For example, fifteen minutes of breathing meditation can help prepare you for a peaceful day or, done at night, for a restful sleep. During the day you might want to check in with your breathing at least once an hour. An alarm watch can provide a helpful reminder: Just breathe when you hear the beep.

Especially remember this game when you "don't have time to catch your breath." Says who? Do exactly the opposite—pause and take a breather. Let the breath be there to help you focus when scattered, and to calm you when you begin to get stressed.

Helpful Hints

Stick with it. Working with the breath can at times seem tedious. It's not as glamorous and fun as some other games. Stick with it anyway. Many of the benefits of this game, like that of #26 "The Witness Protection Program," are cumulative. Over time, as we learn to breathe with depth and awareness, we gain a most precious gift. We've a stress-reducing, health-preserving, soul-enhancing method, ever available and absolutely free.

Mix and match. This game teaches three separate breathing techniques. Nevertheless, you can creatively combine them. For example, you might use simple awareness of your breath as a way to check for, and switch to, belly-breathing. This, in turn, is a good way to breathe in scads of golden light, so mix and match these methods as you like. You may also read about or invent some more. For example, you can vary the color of your imagined light; perhaps use green for healing, orange for energy, blue for illuminating the soul.

Related Readings

Robert Aitken. *Taking the Path of Zen.* San Francisco: North Point Press, 1982. A respected teacher's step-by-step introduction to the Zen practice of breathing meditation.

Thich Nhat Hanh. *The Miracle of Mindfulness: A Manual of Meditation.* Boston: Beacon Press, 1975. The role of breathing in daily mindfulness is discussed by this Buddhist monk. (For a simplified version, see also his *Peace Is Every Step*, and Jon Kabat-Zinn's *Wherever You Go, There You Are.*)

28. About Face!

Invert the elements, and you will find what you seek.

—Anonymous, *The Book of Alze*

◦───◦

ost religions recognize a process of inner reversal as key to spiritual breakthrough. Whether called "conversion," "turning," "repenting," or being "born again," one's previous values are knocked topsy-turvy. Where before one was obsessed with self, now service to God or neighbor becomes the focus. Where material desires once reigned supreme, now spiritual values rule. In alchemical texts, like that one from which the above quote is taken, the "inversion of elements" serves as a symbol of this inner transformation. Even the soul's base elements can be converted into gold.

A soul-turning of this depth is a precious experience. But we can seek mini-versions in our ordinary life. We've all had the experience of turning around a bad day through reversing some unproductive mood or behavior. A well-timed joke dissolves the picnic-from-hell into healing laughter. An honest apology rescues the date-of-a-thousand-blunders. But how to cultivate such metamorphoses?

Today, notice whenever things are circling the drain. You may be sinking into self-loathing, or depression, or a foul and angry mood. (Maybe it feels like you should hang "Beware of Attack Dog" around your neck.) Or, perhaps you're starting to rush faster and faster, or to procrastinate on a needed chore.

Whatever the problem is, stop and tell yourself, "About Face!" Think of old army movies: Upon command all the recruits facing one way suddenly reverse direction. Similarly, you're now reversing thoughts or actions that had you faced the wrong way.

How to accomplish this turn around? Just do it. Practice the exact opposite of what you've been engaged in. Procrastinating? Say "About Face!" and get on with the task. Too rushed? Say "About Face!" and slow to a leisurely pace. Self-hating as you brood on some mistake of the morning? About Face! Let it go. Think of something positive you did.

Busy scrapping with your spouse over who'll drive the kid to the dentist? About Face! Say, "I'll take him." You were getting selfish. Besides, it's hardly worth the fight. Tired and grumpy? About Face! Claim hidden resources of energy (they're in there somewhere) and try to spread a little cheer.

For the fun of it, you might see how many About Faces you can record during the day. In one column ("Before") list the negative thoughts and behaviors you were addressing, and in another column ("After"), the results of your reversal. You might also give yourself an award, as in #3 "My Award-Winning Day," for the day's most dramatic turnaround.

You might encounter some disappointments along the way if an About Face has limited results. Don't beat yourself up (or if you start doing so, About Face that!). The goal of the game is some improvement, not perfection. In the old army movies the new recruits attempting an about face might get their feet crossed a bit and stumble. So might you as you attempt the maneuver. That's okay. Before you were facing entirely the wrong way; now you're headed in a better direction.

Helpful Hints

Get physical. In addition to saying "About Face!" inside your head, it can help to act it out physically. Swivel around your chair. Turn a desk figurine from left to right. Or, if walking, you can imagine a trip wire ahead that reverses polarities: "The moment I reach that tree half-a-block up, I'll reverse my sour mood." Sounds hokey, but it can help.

Before about-facing, there may be something you have to face about it. Finding yourself in an angry or fearful mood, you say "About Face!" and . . . nothing happens. Are you or the game a failure? Not exactly. But there may be something tying up your energies that needs more patient untangling than the original game provides. So reverse the about face into a face about. What do you need to face about the situation and work through in order to get free? Maybe your anger towards another needs an application of forgiveness, or an admission of your own wrongdoings (see #9 "Unpointing the Finger"). Maybe a mounting fear needs to be countered by a good session of faith-filled prayer. When you've faced these things directly, you can better accomplish your About Face!

Willingness is key. If you find an About Face going nowhere, you might also ask yourself, "Am I *willing* to change?" Anger may fill you with a sense of power. Are you willing to give it up? Or you can soak in self-pity like a hot bath. Are you willing to climb out and towel off? If not, you may need to pray for the willingness. We can't About Face successfully if the truth is we don't want to.

Related Readings

Martin Buber. *The Way of Man According to the Teaching of Hasidism.* New York: Citadel Press, 1963. A brief but eloquent introduction to the Jewish notion of the "turning," whereby a wandering or misdirected life is set back on its path.

William James. *The Varieties of Religious Experience: A Study in Human Nature.* New York: Penguin, 1982. A classic overview of the psychology of spirituality, with a detailed discussion of conversion experiences.

29. A Word to the Wise

If you like, you can have this reaching out [toward God], wrapped up and enfolded in a single word. So as to have a better grasp of it, take just a little word. . . . Such a one is the word "God" or the word "love." Choose which one you prefer, or any other according to your liking. . . . Fasten this word to your heart, so that whatever happens it will never go away.

—Anonymous, *The Cloud of Unknowing*

It's easy to overlook the power of words. But think of the impact that a word of cruelty or kindness can have on your mental state. Each word is like an energy-filled power pack that can transform your thoughts, moods, and actions. This power is recognized in the quote above from a classic of Western mysticism.

Today, select a single word to shape your experience. Choose carefully: This word will form an intimate companion for the day ahead. It might represent some virtue you wish to cultivate, like "courage" or "patience." Or perhaps your word speaks to a state of mind. Short on sleep, you use the word "energy," or for a rushed day you select the word "calm." Your word choice can range from the sublimely spiritual to the slightly silly, but it should express a genuine desire of your heart.

Once you have your word, let it sink in and surround you in a variety of ways. Get the linguistic left brain in gear by looking your word up in a dictionary and pondering the definitions you find. It's surprising the insights this can yield. You might also make a list of words related to yours by a common root and meaning. For example, if using the word "joy," think, too, of what it means to "enjoy" an activity, or to be a "joyful" person.

Draw your special word on a piece of paper to post prominently as a reminder. Give this project some pictorial flair; it gets your holistic right brain into the act. For example, the word "*JOY!*" might be drawn in bright swirling colors and embroidered with stars. You could also sketch a scene (no artistic genius required) that expresses your word, like a figure dancing joyfully in an open field.

Throughout the day use your word, and associated words if you wish, as an inner mantra you repeat in your mind. (See #23 "Plugging In.") Perhaps you're stuck on hold waiting to speak to your claims adjuster. Aaarghh. Use your words, "joy, joy, joy," to dissipate mounting frustration. (It may not work perfectly, but it's probably better than "aaarghh.") When possible also use your word, and its relatives, in speech. "How'd your presentation go yesterday?" you're asked. "Well . . . I certainly *enjoyed* getting it over with."

Seek to let your word influence your choices and activities. What *joyous* piece of music could you listen to in the evening? (Perhaps "Joy to the World" or Beethoven's "Ode to Joy"?) How might you make your time with the kids a little more *enjoyable* for everyone? In such ways let this word be your guardian angel, guiding and helping you through the day.

Helpful Hints

Share the wealth. Don't just keep your word clutched to yourself. Seek to radiate its positive energy outward. If, for example, you're working with "strength," see if you can strengthen and empower those you meet. Any word's riches will grow for you as you share the wealth with others.

165

Stick or switch. If you continue with this game, you might stick with one word for several days. The quality it names may need time for gradual cultivation. On the other hand, you might switch words each day (or even within a day) in response to changing inner and outer needs. Say, on Friday you choose "determination" to better cope with a series of surly clients. On the weekend you might switch to a word like "serenity" to gather in some sabbath like rest.

Assemble a spiritual dictionary. Over time, you might consider starting in a loose-leaf notebook a sort of spiritual dictionary, with a page or two devoted to each word. Write down a dictionary definition, what the word means to you, and how it manifests in your life. Perhaps pen a brief poem which includes your word, or copy from a book of quotations some apt usages. You can also fold into the journal your illustration, and other evocative images or mementos. For example, for the word "peace," you might add a photo and a dried flower that remind you of a peaceful weekend in the country. Then at any time you can flip through your dictionary to find the word that best meets your needs.

Related Readings

Byllye Avery. *An Altar of Words: Wisdom, Comfort, and Inspiration for African American Women.* New York: Broadway Books, 1998. The author explores, one by one, a series of inspirational words; for example, the *B*s include "balance," "beauty," "blessings," and "boogie down."

Herbert Benson with Miriam Z. Klipper. *The Relaxation Response.* New York: Avon Books, 1975; and Herbert Benson with William Proctor. *Beyond the Relaxation Response.* New York: Berkley Books, 1984. In the first book cited, this Harvard physician explores the health benefits of a simple meditation practice using a repeated word. In the second book he discusses as well the import of the faith factor—choosing a word or brief mantra consonant with one's deepest beliefs.

30. UNSELfING YOURSELF

We are in training to be nobody special. And it is in that nobody-specialness that we can be anybody. The fatigue, the neurosis, the anxiety, the fear, all come from identifying with somebody-ness. . . . For when we become nobody, there is no tension, no pretense, no one trying to be anyone or anything, and the natural state of the mind shines through unobstructed. The natural state of the mind is pure love, which is not other than pure awareness.

—Ram Dass and Stephen Levine, *Grist for the Mill*

So often our thoughts are dominated by self-concern. How am I doing, feeling, appearing? What will I get out of my activities today in the way of love or money? What do others think of . . . ME? We need not be overly embarrassed about this narcissism. It's part of the human condition, then intensified by a culture that rewards personal success.

Yet spiritual advancement often involves reversing that tendency. To make room in our heart for others, the divine, and the joys of the moment, we must lessen that persistent self-focus.

Today, do a little unselfing. Whenever you notice your thoughts winding back upon the self, use this as a cue to redirect attention outward: to the task at hand, the needs of others, gratitude toward God, or any other positive focus external to ME, MYSELF, and I.

This will not always come easily. Say a work project is handed you that you think belongs on someone else's desk. Immediately, the inner grumbling starts: "I shouldn't have to take on this job. . . . My supervisor does this to me all the time." Your mind becomes a whirlpool of thoughts and emotions circling inward. Like a toilet.

Pause to flush away the self. Absenting your feelings and drives for the moment, ask, "What would be most useful?" Perhaps tackling the task—it's not that big a deal, and an opportunity to be of service. Or you may choose to speak to your supervisor because this will help the office better function. Either way, try to avoid SELF being the goal of your actions and the preoccupation of your thoughts.

All through the day there will be temptations to refocus on yourself. You do a kindly act and want praise and recognition. You grow preoccupied with remorse for one of your mistakes. A success invites you to gloat over your accomplishments. An unexpected problem triggers self-centered fears. Tired and frustrated, you sink into a morass of self-pity.

But whenever you notice self returning, whether in a positive or negative mode, remind yourself again to unself. Success?—thank you, God. Mistake?—the planet will survive. Tired and self-piteous?—my kids need me, I'll find the energy. Yes, especially if I unself.

For fun, you might see how many times throughout the day you can remember to do this. Three times, five times, ten? Of course, patting yourself on the back is hardly the point of the game. Still, we're not ascended masters yet. Until fully unselfed we can use the encouragement provided by noting positive results.

You might also apply this game to long-standing issues in your life that seem tangled up in self. Perhaps you've an ongoing fear, grievance, or point of indecision. To cut through the mess, try subtracting the self. As a result, your perspective may enlarge.

Helpful Hints

Use imagery. If it appeals, you can use mental imagery to help unself. For example, you might think of the ego-self as not being the True You (child of God, divine soul), but a kind of surface garment you don to make yourself "attractive" and "protected" in the midst of a competitive world. To unself, visualize yourself taking this jacket off. Mentally drape it on the back of your chair or hang it out of the way in a closet. There, isn't that a little more comfortable?

Avoid that one-letter word. Instead of worrying about four-letter words, we might pay more attention to a one-letter word that dominates so many conversations—*I*. It can be a struggle to hear another using it without grabbing it back: "*I* know what you mean. It reminds me of something *I* was just thinking on *my* way to work."

There's nothing wrong with sharing of yourself. But today practice the discipline of listening to others and focusing on their needs.

Don't sell yourself short. There's a danger to the unself game: that you might use it as a tool to dim self-awareness, repress emotions, or to let yourself be abused. Perhaps someone has blown off your luncheon appointment. Trying immediately to unself may not bring true resolution. If so, take the time or actions to work things through. "I'm really ticked off. I've got to acknowledge that. I'm going to call the person, find out what happened, maybe mention that I was distressed." Having done that you can better let the incident go, and get back to your unselfing.

If you habitually put yourself down or neglect your needs, be especially careful with this game. As addressed in the "Loving the Self" section of this book, spirituality also involves proper self-care. You might wish to start with those games before returning to this one. Paradoxically, the healthier our sense of self, the better we can unself to focus on others.

Related Readings

Stephen Clissold. *The Wisdom of St. Francis and His Companions*. New York: W.W. Norton, 1978. See this or other accounts of St. Francis, for an example of the joy and love that can result from a truly unselfed life.

Huston Smith. *The World's Religions: Our Great Wisdom Traditions*. San Francisco: HarperSanFrancisco, 1991. This classic exposition suggests how the world's religions each teach different methods to unself.

171

Part Seven
The WONDER of
CREATION

many of the preceding games have addressed the inward spirit. Through prayer, imagery, meditation, and focused acts, we've sought inner joy and freedom.

But the Divine is far more than a pleasant personal experience. He/She/It is arrayed in splendor throughout the universe. Astronomers estimate that this universe contains some fifty billion galaxies, each composed of fifty to one hundred billion stars. Awesome. By comparison, a human life is a humble thing. Yet we're also elevated by our participation in this grandeur. The very carbon in our bodies was forged from atoms fused by exploding supernovas. We're stardust, now somehow endowed with sight and gazing back upon the stars. Orbiting one of these stars is our own home, the earth, a green and blue haven for burgeoning life. We associate miracles with the supernatural. Yet ordinary nature is itself miraculous, changing water to wine each day.

There's a strain of religious thought that would minimize such matters. The world is viewed as a fallen place, the human body but a breeding ground for lust and sin. We're struggling to free the soul from the prison of the physical.

Happily, this view is challenged in a number of sacred traditions. Native American spirituality has always revered nature. "The Great Spirit is the life that is in all things—all creatures and plants and even rocks and the minerals" (Rolling Thunder). This view prevails, as well, in traditional African culture, indigenous peoples the world over, and contemporary Goddess spirituality. It also finds expression in many strains of mainstream Western and Eastern religions. As the Buddha said, "If you wish to know the Divine, feel the wind on your face and the warm sun on your hand."

Often, though, we don't. Rendered oblivious by our busy agendas, we barely notice wind, sun, stars, trees, birds, and soil, or the subtle connection that bind these to one another and to our natural bodies. This inattention weakens our spirit. It also endangers our earth. That which we cease to hold sacred we're far more likely to destroy.

But let's not sink into depression. Better, instead, to play ourselves back into appreciation and wonder. The games that follow are about reawakening to creation: to the beauty, wisdom, and mystery of our own body, and of the natural world. As we do so, we also reawaken to the Source. In the words of medieval mystic Meister Eckhart, "If the soul could have known God without the world, the world would have never been created." Yet, thankfully, blessedly, it was.

31. ENTERING the MIND of NATURE

Let's sit down here, all of us, on the open prairie, where we can't see a highway or a fence. Let's have no blanket to sit on, but feel the ground with our bodies, the earth, the yielding shrubs. Let's have the grass for a mattress, experiencing its sharpness and its softness. Let us become like stones, plants, and trees. Let us be animals, think and feel like animals. . . . A good way to start thinking about nature, talk about it. Rather talk to it, talk to the rivers, to the lakes, to the winds as to our relatives.

—John (Fire) Lame Deer and Richard Erdoes, *Lame Deer Seeker of Visions*

I rn many indigenous cultures, like those of Native Americans, nature is seen as fully alive. Human awareness is but one of the many forms of intelligence that animate the landscape. The far-sightedness of the eagle; the serenity of a stone; the creativity of the spider spinning a universe in her web—if we but listen, we can hear and learn from all these other beings. The tribal shaman is an expert at this.

He or she channels these natural powers to heal illness and keep the community in balance.

Through this game try to tap into this healing power. First, focus your attention on something in nature. This could be any animal, plant, or an aspect of the landscape like a lake, cloud, or rock. Choose carefully. Let your intuition guide you.

Next, grow sensitive to the subtleties of this being. For example, if working with a tree, you might run your hands along its rough bark, listen to its leaves rustling in the breeze, and admire the intricate pattern of its branches. Act as if this were the first time you've ever encountered this being.

Now, go one step further. Regard this being not just as an object, however fascinating, but as a subject with its own awareness. Put yourself into its place. What does it feel like to be this tree (or cloud, or duck, or river)? To have a root system digging into the moist earth while your arms thrust upwards toward the heavens? Does tree-time feel the same as human-time, or is it slower and cyclical? Explore this other consciousness from within.

Then ask yourself what it has to teach you. Imagine this being as your soul-guide, bearing messages of healing and balance. Are you meant to slow down like the patient tree? To put down stronger roots? To sway more flexibly with the winds of change so that you don't grow brittle and break? Listen to your teacher. Draw on its powers. Enter the mind of nature.

If you play this game for a while, you might choose a new being to work

177

with each day. In this way you can meet a host of friends—animal, vegetable, and mineral—each of which speaks to a different side of yourself.

You might, however, choose to stick mainly with one. A Native American tribe or shaman is often associated with a particular totem animal. Perhaps you can discover your own totem, or at least one for this time in your life.

Helpful Hints

Use your body. While this game is called "entering the mind of nature," don't forget to bring your body along. If you're working with a flower, feel your petals (hair or fingers) opening to the sun. If you're trying to commune with Fido, get down on all fours. The world looks very different from a dog's-eye view.

Use art. A way to track and enhance your experience is to record it artistically. Say you're communing with the bird who nests outside your door. Try writing about bird-mind (perhaps in the first-person tense) through evocative prose or poetry. Or, if they are more your media, try capturing the spirit in a watercolor, dance, or musical improvisation. (Don't worry about whether your artwork is good enough. The focus here is on deepening awareness.)

Use reminders, and the thing itself. In addition to your art, you can use other reminders to keep your natural being present. For example, if you've chosen to work with the beach, you might keep a sea stone or a favorite beach photo on your desk. When stressed, play a tape of soothing ocean sounds.

Of course, nothing beats the thing itself. Return to that beach (or tree, or whatever you've chosen) when in need of spiritual renewal.

Related Readings

Robert Bly, ed. *News of the Universe: Poems of Twofold Consciousness.* San Francisco: Sierra Club Books, 1980. A wonderful collection of poems, classical and contemporary, that address the natural world.

John Seed et al. *Thinking Like a Mountain: Towards a Council of All Beings* (Philadelphia: New Society Publishers, 1988). A collection of readings, meditations, poems, and guided fantasies, designed to help us recover our connection to the living earth.

Henry David Thoreau. *Walden or, Life in the Woods.* New York: Vintage Books, 1991. A classic account of two years spent in the woods by a keen observer of, and participant in, the mind of nature. (For a more contemporary wilderness saga, try Anne LaBastille's *Woodswoman.* New York: E. P. Dutton, 1991.)

32. Outside In

Every day is a god, each day is a god, and holiness holds forth in time. I worship each god, I praise each day splintered down, and wrapped in time like a husk, a husk of many colors spreading, at dawn fast over the mountains split.

—Annie Dillard, *Holy the Firm*

Often we're oblivious to the day and its weather except for its effects on our plans. Even then we may divide it simplistically into a "good" day or "bad," "too hot" or "too cold." We rely on air conditioners, central heating units, humidifiers and dehumidifiers, electric lighting, storm windows, and a host of other devices to insulate us from the outside. If "each day is a god," we do our best to ignore it.

Today, notice and embrace the day. Assume the weather is not "too" anything, but just perfect, just as it's meant to be. Whether sunny or rainy, sweltering or frigid, seek to appreciate it to the utmost. Today's weather is a unique planetary mood that never will be exactly repeated. Honor this brief god before it departs.

As often as possible, but at least three times during the day—once in the morning, afternoon, and evening—step outside in a worshipful state of mind. Spend a few minutes simply becoming aware of the day. Notice the texture of the air, the shifting patterns of sun and cloud, of wind and stillness. We're often taught to seek God through interior prayer. Today, instead, hear Spirit speaking all around you in the great outdoors.

Contemplate the day's unique gifts. Blistering sun? Sense the energy pouring onto the planet sustaining all living things. Rainy day? A drink for the parched earth. How delightful it is that water—cooling, cleansing, life-giving—falls like manna from the skies.

Any day, of course, is not a single thing but a story, a lifetime, unfolding in twenty-four hours. Appreciate its morning advent, its settling into midday, its slow descent into darkness opening up the vault of stars.

Also seek out the day's graces meant just for you. Think of the unfolding day as a god, or a friend, or an emissary of Spirit, come to assist you with special messages and moods. Perhaps you're ricocheting through a busy week, and the day's restful, cloudy sky brings you peace. In a funk? A bright sky announces in sunrise and birdsong, "Cheer up. This is no day to be sad." A breeze ruffling your hair, whispers of freedom: "Let go. Throw your troubles to the wind."

One problem should be mentioned. Most of us don't live in pine forests or open fields. When you step outside to appreciate the day, you might be overwhelmed by tall buildings, a cacophony of honking, and the stench of truck exhaust fumes. Three points to make here: 1) If possible go somewhere nice, such as a park, for your outside-in session. 2) If not, remember that even in the midst of human encroachments, nature still lives. Focus on the sky, the weather, a solitary birdsong rather than garbage trucks. 3) If the human intrusions bother you, that's not necessarily a bad thing. We need to be sensitive to the ways we violate the earth. The more we let the outside in, the more we'll wish to guard its beauty.

Helpful Hints

Celebrate through art. As with other games in this section, you may wish to deepen your experience through giving it creative expression. For example, a Japanese seventeen-syllable haiku often captures a single moment in nature (a frog jumping in an ancient pond, a cloud covering the sun) that has emotional or spiritual resonance. You might write a morning, afternoon, and evening haiku celebrating the changing moods of the day.

Celebrate through ritual. Arising early in the morning, you might greet the new day with a bow and outstretched arms. At dusk, you might thank the setting sun for blessings it bestowed. Through such small rituals, you can better "worship each god" and let "holiness hold forth in time."

Reach for the sky. So often we attend to our worldly business oblivious to the magnificent pageant unfolding above our heads. It's called the sky. What Rembrandt painting could rival this art-work of shifting form, light, and color? So look up. (Even in a city the sky's still to be had, though sliced into ribbons.) Lift your eyes and spirit to the heavens.

Related Readings

Phil Cousineau, ed. *The Soul of the World: A Modern Book of Hours.* San Francisco: HarperSanFrancisco, 1993. A magnificent collection of photographs and spiritual excerpts keyed, as in a medieval prayer book, to the hours of the day.

The Earth Works Group. *50 Simple Things You Can Do to Save the Earth.* Berkeley, CA: Earth Works Press, 1989. A handy little manual for how to do our own small part in saving an imperiled planet.

Elizabeth Roberts and Elias Amidon, eds. *Earth Prayers: From Around the World, 365 Prayers, Poems, and Invocations for Honoring the Earth.* San Francisco: HarperSanFrancisco, 1991. A rich collection drawing on diverse authors and cultures.

Clark Strand. *Seeds from a Birch Tree: Writing Haiku and the Spiritual Journey.* New York: Hyperion, 1997. How to write haiku as a spiritual method for opening to self and nature.

33. COMING to OUR SENSES

A sensual spirituality praises the gifts of one's senses—fingers and eyes, ears and olfactory nerves, tongue and imagination, nerves and brain waves and the Gift-giver . . . the keener and keener development of [the senses] leads to a deeper and richer, more sensitive and expansive spiritual experience.

—Matthew Fox, *Whee! We, Wee All the Way Home:*
A Guide to Sensual, Prophetic Spirituality

t oday, come to your senses. You say you haven't lost them? Think again. Or rather, *stop thinking.* We can get so absorbed in our mind-chatter that we lose touch with our sensory experience. We miss out on the richness of our own body, of the world around us, and of its Joyful Creator.

Begin by setting aside some ten to thirty minutes just to come to your senses. If possible, seek out a natural environment inviting to body and spirit. It need not be pristine wilderness. Time relaxing in your back-yard, or a walk down tree-lined streets, can do the trick quite nicely.

Now explore your senses, one by one. For example, you might begin with hearing. Close your eyes (if you're walking, peek now and then) and for a couple of minutes become "all ears." How many sounds can you hear? Bird calls, each with its own tune; the gentle rustling of leaves; the thrum, rising then falling, of a car driving by; a solitary child's voice laughing in the distance. Allow yourself to dissolve into this aural land-scape. Experience the ecstasy of sound.

Now go on to the tactile world. "Get in touch" with yourself and the world. If walking, feel the slight breeze created by your own movement. Sense it trailing through your fingers and tingling your face. Feel the air's temperature washing over you, and your body's sensual response. Experience the contraction and thrusting of your muscles as you stride forward. Do your feet enjoy the pavement or long for the softness of grass?

When done, go on to yet another sense. You might combine taste and smell, so closely linked. Perhaps leave vision for the last since we're so used to relying on it. Even here, don't sink into a taken-for-granted world, but see things anew. Notice small details (shiny stones embedded in the sidewalk, different shades of green in the trees) that ordinarily you'd overlook.

Having explored each sense one by one, now open them all up

together. It's as if you'd first picked out the different instruments of an orchestra—flutes, piano, violins—but now take in the whole symphony. As you do so, permit your attention to float free. You might be startled by the rude squawk of a jay, the sheer blue of the sky, or the odor of someone's breakfast cooking. It's all part of the sensory symphony.

When this exercise is over, you may begin to close down. It's only natural. But throughout the day, as often as you remember or wish, return to one or more senses. Try to celebrate each at some appropriate moment. At lunch, put down the newspaper to focus on your food. (You may feel so filled up by the intensified tastes and smells that you actually need to eat less.) At day's end, don't just carelessly toss off your shoes. Enjoy the feeling as your toes wiggle free. If you put on a piece of music, don't just make it a distant background. Pause to savor the richness of sound.

Come to your senses, even if it means going out of your mind.

Helpful Hints

Get to know your likes and dislikes. When you come to your senses, not all your experiences will be pleasant. For example, you might return from your sense-opening walk to a cluttered, under-lit, slightly odor-ridden room. Suddenly, it bothers you. That's okay. When more in touch with your likes and dislikes you can reshape your environment accordingly. (Clean your room.) Of course, you don't always have total control, but there's usually something you can do. For example, a vase and fresh flower on your office desk might do wonders for a sterile workplace.

188

Give your senses gifts. To awaken your senses in a fun way, offer them special gifts. Remember especially those senses you tend to neglect. Sniff some lavender oil. Pop a sweet-pungent lemon drop. Take a hot bath with soothing salts. Afterwards, invite your partner to . . . Anyway, you get the idea.

Sense the Spirit. Sometimes we think of the soul as divorced from the body, but this can do harm to both. If you attend a house of worship, be aware of the vaulted ceilings or simple wooden pews; stained glass or beckoning darkness; music or meditative silence.

Allow your surroundings to touch your soul. Do this, too, when meditating or praying at home. Search out the proper room, lighting, sacred objects, and body posture to deepen your contemplative experience.

Related Readings

Diane Ackerman. *A Natural History of the Senses.* New York: Vintage Books, 1990. An engaging look at the history, biology, and psychology of the senses, contemplated one by one.

Matthew Fox. *Whee! We, Wee All the Way Home: A Guide to Sensual, Prophetic Spirituality.* Santa Fe: Bear and Company, 1981. The author criticizes ascetic-style religion, arguing for a sensual spirituality that finds God in the wonder of creation.

34. The ARTIST'S EYE

Listen, God love everything you love—and a mess of stuff you don't.
But more than anything else, God love admiration.
You saying God vain?, I ast.
Naw, she say. Not vain, just wanting to share a good thing. I think
it pisses God off if you walk by the color purple in a field somewhere
and don't notice it.

—Alice Walker, *The Color Purple*

remember how as a child you pretended to be different people? One day you were an astronaut, another day a nurse, a cowboy, or a scientist. Such games were not simply acts of self-delusion. You were trying on different selves, experimenting with alternate ways of being. In time, some fell away as uninteresting or unrealistic. In other cases, imaginary play was a step toward developing real powers.

This game is about developing awareness and sensitivity, especially to the beauty of the world. So why not do so by playing pretend? Today, imagine you are a great artist. You can be any sort you choose: a photographer, painter, poet, prose writer, dancer, composer, or filmmaker. Whatever identity you select, enter it at times during the day. For those moments, encounter the world as an artist might. Notice that color purple, and the other simple wonders we so often overlook. It's a way to extend the previous game where we practiced "Coming to Our Senses."

If you're pretending you're a photographer, keep your eye out for possible subjects. You might notice the pattern of light and shade cast by a picket fence. It would make a great black-and-white. Perhaps an old woman walks by. Her age-worn face embodies a ragged beauty. Snap the photograph in your mind.

Or as a writer, note details that could help sketch out her character for a short story. Her stooped posture and limp suggest the ravages of time. Yet she wears a brightly colored scarf, showing the life that still burns within.

Or perhaps you've chosen to be a filmmaker. Going for a walk on a breezy day, you notice vignettes of the wind that would make a beautiful montage; a brown paper bag blown end over end; a flag snapping; passers-by clutching at their hats. Revel in the swirling, grand dance.

You probably can't maintain this keen awareness all day long. Even great artists don't. But during the day, choose two or three times, or more, to gaze through the artist's eye. Don't necessarily wait for a scene of special beauty. What detail might a poet capture about your office? (The books slouching like tired soldiers on your shelf?) What might a painter notice about your face in the mirror? (The left side looks a little sadder than the right?) The world comes alive in a whole new way when seen through the artist's eye.

Helpful Hints

Go with, or against, your strength. If you already work in a particular art form, whether expert or a dabbler, you might wish to play in that mode. But you can also "cast against type." Perhaps you're adept with words but not very visually oriented. You might choose to be a painter to develop that underused sense.

Don't hesitate to switch identities. You may have chosen a particular role (say a writer), but stumble upon a scene that would make a striking photograph. If you like, switch. Re-imagine yourself into whatever sort of artist could best do justice to the scene.

Changing identities can also help revitalize the game if you play it more than once. Be a songwriter today, a filmmaker tomorrow. The world will show forth different sides.

Inspire yourself with art. Before or during this game you might use the artworks of others as inspiration. For example, you might prepare yourself to be a painter by scanning through a favorite artbook. Notice how an old master sees the world, or an impressionist, or a photorealist. Then you can better see the world as they might. Or if playing a poet, you might read some vivid poems of the everyday world. This can help you awaken to life's odd and touching details you otherwise would miss.

While you're at it, you could also produce some artworks yourself—photos, lines of poetry, whatever—inspired by your imagined identity. Don't worry if you feel you've little talent in this area. We can't all be Leonardo da Vincis. But something of the artist's eye is available to us all.

Related Readings

Julia Cameron. *The Artist's Way: A Spiritual Path to Higher Creativity.* New York: Jeremy P. Tarcher/Putnam, 1992. A workbook for twelve weeks of self-transforming exercises and activities designed to unlock your creativity.

Annie Dillard. *Pilgrim at Tinker Creek.* New York: HarperCollins, 1974. A poetic exploration of the natural landscape, including a section on the heightened perception the author calls "seeing."

Frederick Franck. *The Zen of Seeing: Seeing/Drawing as Meditation.* New York: Vintage Books, 1973. This book teaches seeing and drawing as a way to enrich our awareness of the extraordinary (ordinary) world.

35. LISTENING to YOUR BODY

*Behind your thoughts and feelings, my brother, there
stands a mighty ruler, an unknown sage—whose name is self. In your
body he dwells; he is your body.
There is more reason in your body than in your best wisdom.*

—Friedrich Nietzsche, *Thus Spoke Zarathustra*

verywhere you go your body goes too. In many ways, you *are*
your body. Desires, emotions, and needs well up from your
physical base. Your very life is sustained by its age-old wisdom
regulating a thousand physiological processes to a finely tuned homeo-
stasis. So, there's nothing you know better, no one with whom you are
more intimate, than your own body—right? Not necessarily.

In the modern Western world, we've largely lost touch with our body.
Our culture has taught us to suppress, control, and transcend its calls in

a multitude of ways. Our body longs for a walk in the sunshine; we plunk it down in a stiff chair. We spend hours typing words on a computer screen when we might rather dance and sing. Exhausted, we force ourselves awake. In need of nutritious food, we gobble down junk. A murmur of lust, anger, or joy ripples through the body, and we tell it in no uncertain terms to go away. Our mind has other plans.

Today, seek to recover your body's voice. Listen carefully, even prayerfully, to what it has to teach you.

Begin by thinking of your body as your best friend. After all, you do spend your whole life together. Imagine that your body wishes to take care of you, and for you to take good care of it.

As you go through the day, keep asking your body two simple questions. First, "How are you doing?" Second, "What do you want?"

"How are you doing?" For a full-bodied answer, explore what's going on inside. Are your muscles relaxed, or tightened in stress? Are you feeling energetic, ready to grab the tiger of the day by the tail? Or are you still a bit sleepy: Tiger, go away! Is a chronic injury acting up, a headache coming on, or are you feeling (dare to say it) pretty darn good? And how does your body like the day's weather? The clothes you've picked out? The breakfast you have planned?

You might find that your body likes, above all else, simply being asked such questions. It shows that someone cares enough to reverence its experience.

Let the first question: "How are you doing?" lead naturally to the second: "What do you want?" Imagine the body telling you of its needs and desires. Some requests may be simple. "I'd like a couple of aspirin for this headache. No reason to wait until it's worse." Or, "Please, please, please, let's get up from this chair and take a stretch. I've been sitting here too darn long." Or, "I'm exhausted. How about we get to a bed at a reasonable hour tonight?" Commonsense stuff. But that doesn't mean you always operate in accordance. Today, do. Listen to your body and, when possible, act on its advice.

Throughout the day you might find your body making creative suggestions that subtly alter your habits. "Sure, it's shower time, but wouldn't it be nice instead to luxuriate in a hot bath?" Or, "Let's go for a brisk walk this morning. I'm tired of being a slug." Or, "I hate the fluorescent light in this office. Please bring in a desk lamp. And how about a nice poster for that bare wall?" You may find your body has a deeper appreciation of the world, and your own best interests, than does your one-track mind.

Playing this game over time may help you clarify what you most need to be happy and healthy. How much exercise, relaxation, sleep, contact with beauty, should be part of your daily routine? Don't worry if you can't adhere to this plan perfectly. The world often doesn't cooperate. Nor do we always follow through on our good intentions. Still, having a plan is an important first step.

While befriending your body, don't forget to express gratitude. "Thanks for carrying me through another day in good health. Thanks for the arms with which I hug my child, the eyes with which I saw the sunrise."

If you're uneasy about something, don't hesitate to bring it up. "@!%*?# knee, why do you keep giving me problems?" Or, "Body, you just don't seem as strong as you used to be. Could it be we're getting old?" Imagine what your body might reply. Maybe something like, "Yep, we're not twenty years old anymore. Can't do some things we once did. But you learn your limits, you adjust. There's a lot of life to be lived." Yes, and it's a better life when you're listening to your body.

197

Helpful Hints

Hear your body, but don't always obey. Just because your body makes a suggestion doesn't mean you have to submit. Asking what your body wants right now, perhaps its answer is "to bust someone in the jaw," or "hot sex, immediately" or "lots and lots of choco-late!" You have to evaluate which messages are appropriate to pursue and override any that would be destructive.

At the same time, refrain from labeling your cravings dirty or bad. Remember that your body is the product of millions of years of evolutionary wisdom. Without aggression, sex, and the pursuit of chocolate (or other tasty foods), we would hardly have survived. If religiously minded, you might think of your body as God-created and therefore beautiful and good. It's not some mistake that we have a body, but exactly what's meant to be.

Expect wisdom and balance and spirituality. What we hear our body say can also be preshaped by our expectations. As in the above examples, many of us have been taught to associate the body only with "baser instincts" like aggression, lust, and gluttony, all threatening to run wild.

But think instead of your body as a natural seeker of balance. Enough is enough. It wishes food when hungry, but when filled up, wants to stop. It thrives on a proper harmony of exercise and rest, discipline and play, stimulation and tranquility. Listen for messages that help you to find that healthy balance.

Remember, too, as mentioned in #33 "Coming to Our Senses," that the body participates in the movements of Spirit. When praying, listen for the posture your body wants to assume: kneeling humbly, cradling your hands, or stretching joyfully for the heavens? Each can unlock a different experience. So, too, can music, or seated meditation, or movement. Let your body be your spiritual guide.

Ritualize. Another way to care for your body and let it care for you is through the use of healing rituals and ceremonies. On awakening, you might greet your body and give it a loving stretch. A ritual of yoga, or brisk exercise, or even an afternoon catnap, might help it to be at its best. Before sleep, you might relax different parts of your body, or bless each in turn. What rituals are right for you? Ask your body.

Befriend the rejected. There may be certain parts of your body you habitually dislike. You may hate your nose, your height, your thighs, or all of the above. But in harmony with this game, seek to befriend that which you've been taught to reject. Accept this part of your physical self: Try to see its own power, or vulnerability, or beauty. Imagine what it might say to you if it could. And do you owe it an apology, or some words of appreciation? Be willing to call on spiritual help with this issue. It's hard to let go of self-hate.

199

Related Readings

Mirka Knaster. *Discovering the Body's Wisdom*. New York: Bantam Books, 1996. An introduction to more than fifty Eastern and Western mind-body practices designed to relieve pain, reduce stress, and foster physical, emotional, and spiritual healing.

Andrew Weil. *8 Weeks to Optimal Health*. New York: Alfred A. Knopf, 1997. A guide to simple practices that cultivate a healthy mind-body, from a leader in the field of complementary medicine.

Part Eight

DANCING with
TIME and
ETERNITY

n order to play the games in this book, something was needed and presupposed. Now is the time to make that explicit—and that thing itself is time. It takes time to experience or accomplish anything in life. After all, what is a life except a bunch of time strung together?

The way in which we use our time has everything to do with our quality of life. We can choose to manage time productively since, we're reminded, "time is money." Conversely, we can "waste time" or "kill time" if we choose. Or we may linger with some enjoyable pastime that literally "passes the time." Our culture sanctions all these options. What it has less to teach us about, however, is the spiritualization of time. In the words of Jewish sage Abraham Joshua Heschel in *The Sabbath*, "The higher goal of spiritual living is not to amass a wealth of information, but to face sacred moments. . . . Spiritual life begins to decay when we fail to sense the grandeur of what is eternal in time."

This section presents a variety of strategies for rediscovering the sacred in time. There are games that invite us to slow down, and to appreciate the here and now. Paradoxically, we may be able to do this better through some imaginary time travel. One game suggests you picture a future self looking back upon the present. Another game has you pretend this is your last day on earth. A final game reverses that premise: What if today were to be repeated eternally? Different in approach, the games share a common purpose. We're not here to kill time, but to savor it and render it holy.

The ending to the book thus leads us back to the beginning in a kind of circular time. Again, we're learning to *celebrate the ordinary,* the focus of the first games. The truth is that nothing's ordinary unless we make it so. Each moment is a door which can open into rooms of magic, love, and transformation. Or that door can lead to some place all too familiar: boring furniture and gray walls.

What's our choice to be?

36. The TAKE-YOUR-TIME TANGO

Constant hurry and day-in, day-out pressure take a cumulative toll on the nervous system. When the hurry becomes chronic, the effects of this toll build up in the mind as well. What begins as nervous tension becomes rigid patterns in the way we think and act. The mind itself gets speeded up; and when the mind gets speeded up it is easily subject to negative emotions like anger and fear. A racing mind is simply moving too fast for love, compassion, tenderness, and similarly quiet states. . . . We cannot get control of our behavior until we get a firm grip on the wheel. And that means we have to learn to slow down our pace of living.

—Eknath Easwaran, *Take Your Time*

Ever seen the tango danced gracefully? It is done to a slow and stately rhythm, lending a careful elegance to each step.

Today, dance through life in this way. Instead of your customary pace (probably too fast if you're a denizen of the modern world), slow down a notch. Do whatever you do in a calm and leisurely fashion. If you have a busy life, there may be a lot on your plate. Yet, as much as possible, don't be driven by inner fear, external deadlines, or rushed companions to stumble through a speeded-up dance. Act as if you have all the time in the world. Come to think of it, you do: No one else has any more hours.

Tango dancers also seem to maintain full concentration on their moves. You can imagine how the dance would deteriorate if they started splitting attention. "Let's see, did I remember to throw that white shirt in the laundry? I need a change of clothes before going out to the restaurant tonight. Did they get our reservation? I better grab the cellular and call in." Meanwhile, steps would be missed and feet trod on.

So in today's slow-dance *do one thing at a time.* Instead of cooking dinner while talking on the phone, wiping the counters, and emptying the dishwasher, devote yourself to just one task, giving it the benefit of your full attention. If you are conversing with someone, really be there. Slicing carrots for dinner? Then do so with care, enjoying the orange circles that your wizardry has created. No rush. No seventeen things at once.

You may find it surprisingly hard to slow down. If so, don't just throw your hands up in despair, but think or write about the reasons. Is it a matter of excessive outer demands, or of inner drivenness? Are you a people-pleaser, terrified of rejection if your performance lessens? Or is there an emotion (sadness, anger, fear) you are trying to escape? Facing such problems can be an initial step toward lessening their hold on your life.

And that life, you may find, only becomes fuller when you start to slow down. Far from wasting time, you'll probably get better work done. Life becomes more peaceful and enjoyable. In fact, the take-your-time-tango is kind of a (quiet) blast.

Helpful Hints

Preparation never hurts. Busy, busy, busy? Don't be a victim. There are certain concrete steps you can take to support a more leisurely day. Get up a little earlier so you're not rushing from the start. Sketch out a daily plan that helps keep you focused and efficient. Let that plan reflect your important priorities. See if there aren't time-wasters and tension-producers you can delegate or (joyful day!) eliminate entirely.

Use music. Music, as we all know, can influence our mood and pace. So throughout the day use soothing music, when possible, to help you calm down. You can also employ the "inner music" of a mantra (see #23 "Plugging In"), or the imagined sound of a tango band to help set a leisurely rhythm.

Downshift, don't slam on the brakes. You're not going to break habits of a lifetime overnight. If you set yourself too lofty goals, you may simply end up feeling a failure. So don't try to screech to a halt from overdrive. Instead, downshift a bit in ways that feel comfortable to you. Notice any little successes which you can then build on tomorrow. That is, be content to slow down slowly.

Shift gears as needed. Using the metaphor of a car shifting gears suggests that your pace need not be uniform. Perhaps there's much to get through at a busy luncheon meeting. Shift up to high gear and step on the gas. The flow of traffic demands it. But afterwards remember to brake and downshift. Otherwise you'll tax your engine through the rest of the day, burning unnecessary fuel. At night, reading to your child, you might downshift even further. Enjoy the leisurely read in first gear before you park your carcass in bed.

Related Readings

Eknath Easwaran. *Take Your Time: Finding Balance in a Hurried World.* New York: Hyperion, 1997. An accessible guide for how to slow down, live in the present, and give time to the important things in life.

Stephan Rechtschaffen. *Timeshifting: Creating More Time to Enjoy Your Life.* New York: Doubleday, 1996. A physician suggests a method to gain "time freedom" by consciously choosing our flow and rhythm, and shifting gears as appropriate.

Elaine St. James. *Simplify Your Life: 100 Ways to Slow Down and Enjoy the Things That Really Matter.* New York: Hyperion, 1994. One way to reduce time pressures is to systematically simplify your life.

37. PRESENT!

*When we can move through life eating, sleeping, working, making love,
without, as we do so, dwelling on the past or in the future, then we can live
with all possible vigor or joy. . . . How refreshing, to live concentratedly in
the instant. To give over regrets, anticipations, worries, reflections, and
reflections on reflections. To focus on the job at hand. How refreshing,
and how loosening of prejudices and inhibitions.*

—Stewart W. Holmes and Chimyo Horioka, *Zen Art for Meditation*

209

remember when your name was called in school roll and you had
to cry out, "Present!"? Well, today announce yourself as "present"
to the people and activities you encounter. Say this word in your
head, or even out loud, when your mind feels scattered or stressed.

For example, you may find you're brooding over the past. "Why did
I get to bed so late? I should have known I'd be exhausted." Well, such
regrets are exhausting, too. Use the thought, "Present," to lay the past to
rest. Reawaken to the here and now.

Use the same thought when you catch yourself wandering, ghostlike, through an imagined future. "I hope my talk next Tuesday goes well. But what if . . ." Stop. Remind yourself gently but firmly, "present." Leave next Tuesday where it belongs—next Tuesday. "Take therefore no thought of the morrow. . . . Let the troubles of the day be sufficient thereof." (Matthew 6:34.)

When reminding yourself, "Present," you might also take a few deep breaths (see #27 "Breathing ABCs"). The simple act of observing your breath can help you calm and center. So, too, does being present itself. Nothing is more stress-producing than cataloguing the dozen things you have to accomplish. Instead, do one thing at a time in the present. The result is more inner peace.

Another thing about using the word *present*—it has a double meaning. It not only refers to the here and now, but is a synonym for gift. Remember this, too, as you think the word. Each moment is a special gift waiting to be unwrapped. This conversation with a friend; the taste of my coffee and muffin; this breeze swirling in the window, rattling the blinds in a dance of light and shadow. How many gifts we discard unopened by being mentally elsewhere! Today, open some of these presents. Don't view the moment as an obstacle to surmount, but a gift to stop and enjoy.

Through this game you might also become aware of when you're naturally more present or absent to your life. View the latter cases as a challenge. Say you're a morning person—alert and raring to go with the sunrise—but by late in the day your body has been taken over by a zombie ("Midafternoon of the Living Dead"?). Try a brief rest, a splash of cold water, and the word present, to re-collect your energy. Or maybe you have a habit of zoning out on emotions like sadness or anger. Instead, try to stay with them. Dare to feel your feelings a bit more. It may not always be pleasurable, yet today be present, not absent, to your life.

Helpful Hints

Give yourself presents. Sometimes the present moment is about as alluring as a pair of smelly sweatsocks. Say you're paying the bills: boring, not to mention stressful. But why not give yourself a present more to your liking? While paying those bills, perhaps pour yourself a nice, cold drink, or put on a piece of your favorite music. A now is a terrible thing to waste. See if it can't be salvaged.

Be present to people. When talking with others our focus often wanders; we're cruising on autopilot. Today, you might practice being a little more present with those who cross your path. If you ask, "How are you?" mean it, and pay attention to the answer. If someone else asks you the same, share a bit more than

211

you might otherwise. It can be scary to open up in this way, but being present is the greatest gift we can offer one another.

Stop, look, and listen. During the day it can be helpful to suddenly startle yourself awake. For example, use a watch alarm that beeps the hour. Whenever it goes off, right then stop, look, and listen. Be present in the moment. Or when driving do the same when you come to a red light. Use the stoppage to pause your flow of thoughts and be right where you are.

212

Related Readings

Thich Nhat Hanh. *Peace is Every Step: The Path of Mindfulness in Everyday Life*. New York: Bantam, 1991. This Vietnamese Buddhist monk gives a series of simple practices for how to use driving, answering the phone, washing dishes, and other everyday acts to summon us back to the present.

Charles T. Tart. *Living the Mindful Life: A Handbook for Living in the Present Moment*. Shambhala Publishers, 1994. Drawing on the teachings of the Middle-Eastern mystic G. I. Gurdjieff, the author presents a series of imaginative techniques for reclaiming the vital *now*.

38. TIME TRAVELING

If you have a flat tire or lock yourself out of your house, what's it going to mean one hundred years from now? How about if someone acted unkindly toward you or if you had to stay up most of the night working? What if your house didn't get cleaned or your computer breaks down? Suppose you can't afford to go on a much needed vacation, buy a new car, or move to a larger apartment? All of these things and most others are brought into a deeper perspective when looked at with a hundred-year view.

—Richard Carlson, *Don't Sweat the Small Stuff . . . and it's all small stuff*

the above quote expresses a sentiment you may have already heard in some form: "It won't make any difference in a hundred years." Yet for some this is not an entirely cheering thought. "Great, in a hundred years I'll be dead, you'll be dead, we'll all be dead. That's supposed to make me feel better?!" The object of such "time travel" is, of course, to recover perspective; taking the long view exposes how many of our daily mountains are but molehills in disguise. On the other hand, taking too long a view can render life's landscape flat.

So pretend you have a time machine that you can set for whenever you choose. It allows you to take a trip in your imagination to any point in the future.

As an example, you might set your time machine for twenty years from now. Then, as you go through the day, try to witness events from that distanced position. You're not simply caught up in the tumults of the moment. Part of you retains the perspective of that person yet to come.

Say you and a friend have a disagreement about what movie you want to go see. You're in the mood for a comedy; he has his heart set on an action thriller. Before the tension crackles, remember to see things through the eyes of that future self. Twenty years from now would you really care which film you'd seen? Would you even remember your choice? Probably not. It's insignificant. But it might have meaning that you were friends with this person. The joy and caring you shared may still be a fond memory, or even an ongoing part of your life. Put your focus there where it belongs. Compromise about the movie or laugh the whole thing off. Arnold Schwarzenegger isn't so bad.

In such ways, use this game as a TUD—a Trivia Unmasking Device. So your child is running late again for school. The weather sucks. You've lost a document you need. The supermarket is out of your favorite brand of cereal. Seen from the future, it's all exposed as trivia—hardly worth the mental anguish.

Also let this game serve as a MUD—a Meaning Unfolding Device. It

214

can recall you to what really matters. Not whether your kid ran late one day, but whether you can accept and support her. Not whether you misplaced a document, but whether you can learn to handle such things with humor, patience, and a dose of self-forgiveness. Otherwise, you may be paying the prices even twenty years from now.

As you time travel, you might experience a paradox. You're imagining yourself in the future looking back on your past. Yet the result is a richer present.

If you like this game, you can also incorporate it into your daily planning. For example, instead of a simple to-do list, you might write "trivial" or "meaningful" next to different items, based on your travel through time. You may still need to attend to certain trivial items (do the laundry; call the repairman). But your items labeled "meaningful" (pray in the morning; stay calm and sane at work) keep you focused on what really matters.

215

Helpful Hints

Visualize your future self. To make this game more concrete, you might visualize that future you. For example, if you've set your time machine for twenty years from now, just how old would you be? Do you think you'd still be working at your current job? How might your circumstances have changed?

In our age-phobic culture, such thoughts may be a bit scary. Yet imagine your future self not as diminished somehow but as having grown in wisdom (see #22 "The Inner Elder"). It's often said, "I wish I could go back and do some things over. I'd have (spent more time with my child, really appreciated life, been more present in a relationship . . .)." But why not draw on this elder insight right now? Use your future self as a spiritual guide. Allow him or her to accompany you through the day, providing you with needed perspective.

216

Fiddle with the dials. You can experiment with different settings on your time machine. If twenty years from now seems unimaginable, you might travel to a nearer future. Ask yourself, will this matter one year from now, or even by next month? It's surprising how many gripping events can't survive that simple test.

Conversely, to keep a major trauma in perspective, you might travel to a hundred years or more from now when the earth will be largely repeopled. Then, too, you can imagine a time machine setting labeled "eternity." Go there when you need to glimpse events from a God's-eye point of view.

You can space-travel, too. When you're disturbed by events in your immediate life or surroundings, it can also help to travel, in your imagination, through the vast reaches of space. Picture the endless ocean. Step outside and survey the stars. You might even write down your "cosmic address," such as:

Jane Thurman
124 Woodlawn Drive
Hanover, CT
U.S.A
Northern Hemisphere
Earth
Solar System
Vicinity of the Orion Arm
Milky Way Galaxy (two hundred billion stars)
The Local Supercluster of Galaxies (radius, one hundred million light-years)
The Universe (fifty billion galaxies)

It kind of keeps our small problems in perspective.

217

Related Readings

Richard Carlson. *Don't Sweat the Small Stuff . . . and it's all small stuff.* New York: Hyperion, 1997. This book by a psychologist and stress-reduction counselor presents one hundred helpful strategies "to keep the little things from taking over your life."

Charles Dickens. *A Christmas Carol.* New York: Pocket Books, 1939. Scrooge's ghosts take him on some time travels that help him discern what is truly of value in life.

39. YOUR LAST,
BEST DAY

*"Death is our eternal companion," Don Juan said with a most serious air.
"It is always to our left, at an arm's length. . . . The thing to do when
you're impatient," he proceeded, "is to turn to your left and ask advice
from your death. An immense amount of pettiness is dropped if your death
makes a gesture to you, or if you catch a glimpse of it, or if you just have
the feeling that your companion is there watching you. . . .
Death is the only wise adviser that we have."*

—Carlos Castaneda, *Journey to Ixtlan*

imagine that today is your last day on earth. Tomorrow you'll be
gone. Suppose that you have some unnamed condition from
which you are about to die. Or if you find this thought too upsetting, simply imagine you're about to leave the earthly plane on a trip to
other regions. Either way, this is the last day you will have to experience
the world and all the people around you.

Rather than sinking into morbid depression, use this thought as your wise adviser. Knowing there is no tomorrow, what opportunities should you seize today? Perhaps *joy* steps forth as something not to be postponed. You decide to go out for a special café lunch rather than gobble down a sandwich at your desk. In the evening, you might put a favorite song on the headphones, switch off the lights, and dance your heart out: You can't wait for some weekend party.

Or perhaps you turn your focus to experiences of love, or beauty, or prayer. Decide what is of most significance to you. Working late at the office, or playing with your child? Crossing items off your to-do list, or having a fun and balanced day? Choose accordingly on this, your last day.

220

Then, too, let this game awaken you to gifts already present in ordinary life. You've barely noticed the last thousand setting suns (ho-hum). It's quite different when this is the last you'll ever see. Observe the orange-streaked clouds lit up in flame, the blue magic of a sapphire dusk settling over the city's houses, their windows lit from within.

Also view as precious each human encounter. Would you wish your final talk with a friend to end in a careless gesture ("Sorry, my phone just rang, gotta go")? If not, then treat the other with care and attention. Remember this will form their last impression of you. And while you're at it, consider if there's unfinished business to clear up. You might apologize to someone you mistreated, or express your love to a family member. If you've the nerve, then do so today.

You can also look at your life's larger patterns. Modify the game slightly: say you had not just a day, but a few months or years left to live. In this limited time, what activities and relationships would you make a top priority? Are there things you want to do which must no longer be postponed? Conversely, are there things you could gladly jettison? They might include outer conditions (that interminable commute!) or inner energy-wasters (worry, petty resentments). Do you really have time for that stuff? Not in your last, best month or year. Maybe it's time for some changes starting today.

Helpful Hints

A little sadness is okay. You might find that this game evokes some sadness as you think of saying good-bye to so much. Let that feeling emerge. If you suppress it, you may also kill off your joy. Yet remember this game is not about generating grief. The focus is less on death's losses than on reclaiming the richness of life.

You need not play "all or nothing." This is a challenging game to play to the max. You may be reluctant to experience the strong emotions and radical acts that might unfold on a real last day. Besides you must attend to ordinary duties. Your boss won't be thrilled if you take off a "death day."

So play to your own level of comfort. Without going all the

221

way, you can still realize benefits. If this game only shapes three or four moments and choices, those alone may transform the day.

There's always tomorrow. You may be disappointed that your last, best day didn't turn out that great. Yet, thankfully, you are not really dying. You can learn from what went wrong and try again tomorrow. You may make progress toward a better day.

Related Readings

Stephen Levine. *A Year to Live.* New York: Bell Tower, 1997. The author plays and presents a provocative game: living the next year of your life as if it were your last. (Also see other books by Levine on the art of conscious living and dying.)

Sogyal Rinpoche. *The Tibetan Book of Living and Dying.* San Francisco: HarperSanFrancisco, 1993. A wonderful overview of the Tibetan tradition, which views the awareness of, and preparation for, death as central to spiritual growth.

Leo Tolstoy. *The Death of Ivan Ilych and Other Stories.* New York: New American Library, 1960. See this classic story of how a very ordinary man is transformed by facing his mortality.

40. The ETERNAL Day

What if some day or night a demon were to steal after you into your
loneliest loneliness and say to you: "This life as you now live it and have
lived it, you will have to live once more and innumerable times more; and
there will be nothing new in it, but every pain and every joy and every
thought and sigh and everything unutterably small or great in your life
will have to return to you, all in the same succession and sequence". . . . If
this thought gained possession of you, it would change you as you are or
perhaps crush you. . . . how well disposed would you have to become to
yourself and to life to crave nothing more fervently than this ultimate
eternal confirmation and seal?

—Friedrich Nietzsche, *The Gay Science*

friedrich Nietzsche, the nineteenth-century German philosopher,
advanced the doctrine of eternal recurrence as a possible truth and
fruitful thought-experiment. Could you bear to live over and over
again your life exactly as it is? (Ouch.) This reverses the premise of

"Your Last, Best Day," yet the two games have much in common. We are shocked awake to the preciousness of time, and the loss when we toss it away.

So imagine that whatever you do or feel today will be infinitely repeated. (If "infinitely" seems a bit overwhelming, substitute "lots of times.") On this basis, give careful thought to your acts. Remember that whatever you choose for breakfast, you will need to eat over and over. Best to select a healthy or pleasurable meal. And consider carefully the greeting you give your partner over coffee. Maybe the norm is a perfunctory grunt (expressing: "Hi. Go away. Life support systems are still fragile"). Understandable. But today you might select a slightly nicer greeting; it will echo down the corridors of time.

If in a rush to work, you start to curse the traffic, pause and reconsider. Do you really want to rush and curse for all eternity? Sounds like purgatory, or the ninth circle of hell. Instead, see if you can't carve out a little slice of heaven. Relax. Turn on some music. You might say a prayer for someone in need. Remember that even a single act of love will be infinitely multiplied.

In such ways, let this game motivate you to value each moment and put it to the best possible use. Of course, there'll be many times you'll sink back into "it's just another Tuesday" consciousness. Simply remind yourself that this is your eternal day. Your thoughts and actions are not to be casually thrown away, but built with care to last.

Of course, no matter what your plan, your day will surely be flawed. (It might even turn into a disaster.) You may then be tempted to brood over failures now eternally multiplied. Stop. That's hardly the point of the game.

Instead, accept whatever comes as a learning experience. You might make a "delights list" noting the day's pleasures and successes, and a "disappointments list" acknowledging what went wrong. Try to learn from the latter. If you play the game repeatedly you may gain insights from the first day that shapes a slightly better day-two, and so on. Thankfully, we retain the ability to change. And growing toward eternity takes time.

225

Helpful Hints

Get a head start. Upon awakening you might give the day ahead careful thought. What experiences would you most like to seek out? Do you wish to focus on fun, prayer, accomplishment, sharing love, or opening to beauty? What is of great enough value to stand the test of repetition?

This moment is the beginning of the rest of your life. Yeah, yeah, we've all heard that cliché. Yet, like many clichés it conceals a rich truth within its musty wrapper. Each moment is a new beginning.

So even if your eternal day gets off to a bad start, start again. And again, and again, if need be. Sooner or later you'll create some special moments worthy of eternal return.

Related Materials

Christopher M. Bache. *Lifecycles: Reincarnation and the Web of Life.* New York: Paragon House, 1990. An introduction to the notion of, and evidence for, reincarnation—the doctrine that suggests we grow toward the eternal through a multiplicity of lives.

Groundhog Day (Columbia/Tristar, 1993). In this lighthearted, but profound comedy, the hero has to live the same day over and over until he learns how to love.

Friedrich Nietzsche. *A Nietzsche Reader,* R. J. Hollingdale, ed. London: Penguin Books, 1977. See works by and about Nietzsche to explore further his notion of eternal recurrence.

EPILOGUE

WHERE DO I GO FROM HERE?

aving played forty games (or some such number) the question naturally arises, "Where do I go from here?" The answers are as various as there are readers. Or maybe there's just one answer: It's up to you.

Still, a few suggestions may prove helpful. If you've enjoyed these games for the soul there are a number of ways to further incorporate them into your life.

One I call the "deep well" approach. If you want to reach spiritual waters, some masters teach, don't dig a dozen shallow wells. All together may yield nothing in the long run. Instead pour your energy into digging one deep well—that is, committing yourself wholeheartedly to a single path or method.

If you're of this mind-set, you might focus future efforts on one or a small number of games. Perhaps the "Breathing ABCs" and "The Witness Protection Program" gave you a sense of freedom. You might seriously pursue Buddhist-style meditation that utilizes such techniques.

Or maybe your heart lit up with more God-centered games like "The (Not So) Imaginary Friend." This alone could be your deep well as, through the joys and sorrows of everyday life, you practice the presence of God

You can also use the model of an exercise program. In our health-conscious times many people are thinking through a personal approach to keeping fit. (That's not to say they necessarily follow it.) Ideally, such a program should be well balanced, exerting different muscles and building up the heart. Just as importantly, it should be fun. We'll hardly keep at it for long if our regimen is unpleasant.

Similarly, you might design a program of soul games that's well balanced and fun to play. For example, you might start each morning with a "Coming to Our Senses" walk, "Thinking to Thank" your body and the universe. During the day you choose to "Golden Rule" at least three people, and to be "Present!" whenever you recall. Before bed, you turn your thoughts to the positive by reviewing your "Award-Winning Day."

Maybe each Wednesday you write a "God Letter" to build your contact with the divine. And on weekends you make sure to practice the "Use of the Useless." It helps you escape that work-driven mind.

If you design such a game program know that you won't (and need not) follow it one hundred percent. Nothing so quickly turns play into work as harsh perfectionism.

Also, be open to change. Perhaps your "Coming to Our Senses" walks, which started out pleasurable, have grown repetitive and boring. Ditch 'em! For a time the Spirit may breathe life into a game, but when it departs you should follow its lead. Seek out a different sort of play that now speaks to your heart. "Enthusiasm," from the Greek word *theos*, literally means "having a god within." Listen for those games that, at any given time, arouse your genuine enthusiasm. They may be the ones in which God now dwells, and be best suited to your spiritual growth.

Of course, this method can fall prey to the "shallow well" criticism. We should be wary of switching practices each time we meet a block or dry spell, or we risk being the perpetual dilettante.

Still, there are merits to free exploration. Ram Dass, the noted spiritual teacher, says, "What's wrong with digging a bunch of shallow wells?" He traveled the world to learn different traditions and techniques, discovering value in each.

Similarly, you might dig shallow wells with gusto. That is, play lots of different games. Rotate them quickly when they grow stale. Inquire each morning what seems like a good focus for the day or week ahead. You won't go far wrong if Spirit helps guide your decisions.

Switching games can also help you respond to life's changing demands. Perhaps you're hobbled unexpectedly by a broken ankle. To deal with it constructively you might dust off "Life's Perfect Lessons." Are there teachings and opportunities to be found even in this handicap? Or, maybe you're having a hard time letting go of a mistake.

Perhaps it's time to apply a dose of "Blessed Imperfection." Forgive yourself. So you made an error. Join the club called the human race.

Then, too, why not make up your own games? There is something absolutely precious and unique about your soul's journey through life. Prepackaged games won't always meet your needs. But thankfully you, too, have access to a divine Gamemaster. He/She/It can supply you with inspiration suited to your own personality and situation. Plus it's simply enjoyable to make up games. Why should I get all the fun?

To assist your thinking, you might ask yourself two questions. The first is: *Right now, in my spiritual journey, what challenges or obstacles do I face?* These might include outer problems, like being in a difficult relationship, unemployed, or under time and money pressures. Or else your challenges may be largely internal: You feel bored, angry, or riddled by fears.

On a more positive note, you might also ask yourself: *Is there anything I particularly feel called to right now, something that would bring peace or joy?* See if you sense an answer. Is this a time to practice generosity, or to withdraw into healing solitude? Do you long for more stability, or to set off on a new adventure?

With these two questions in mind (challenges and calls), design a game that best meets your current needs. It might help you cope with a problem, stimulate progress where you're stuck, or fulfill an inner yen. Whatever, be sure to make your game pleasurable. Give it some structured rules (though these can be amended). Don't aim too high. Make your game clear and doable. You're more likely to experience success.

For example, say you have a bad case of the blahs. It's not that anything is drastically wrong. It's just that amidst all your humdrum routines, life has lost its pizzazz.

You might design a game called "The Delightful Difference" where you alter your day in fun ways. You'll drive to work by a different route, listen to a different radio station, order a different sandwich for lunch, and so on. See if this doesn't wake things up.

Or perhaps you're struggling with a buildup of frustration. You feel disappointed in your mate, your kid, your co-workers. You want them all to change, and have a clear vision of how. Still they go on being just who they are. Meanwhile, you're the one suffering the most.

Why not make up a game of "Letting Go"? Every time you notice a demand arising that people be other than they are, seek to release it. How? That's up to you. You might keep a running list of demands, then crumple and burn it as a symbol of letting go. Or you could examine each situation in turn, and see whether getting your way would really solve all your problems. Probably not. Or maybe you know you need divine aid to let go. Practice handing over each demand in prayer: "Please relieve me of this. Help me to accept people as they are."

The point is there's no one right way to structure a game. Try to intuit what would work best for you. Then experiment and adjust.

Perhaps most important is not how you play, or what you play on any specific day: it's that you play at all—that you continue with games for the soul. In this way, you retain the joy and creativity of a child, even while you spiritually mature. Life may throw hardship and challenges your way. But play on. By all means, play on.

ACKNOWLEDGMENTS

i thank God for this book (literally): for inspiring its basic idea, and the specific games within it—meant as much for my growth as that of any reader.

On the human plane, there are so many others to thank. I am fortunate to teach at Loyola College in Maryland, with wonderful colleagues in the philosophy department, in the Center for Values and Service, and in the school's administration. Not many institutions would have proved so nurturing of my nontraditional work. My students have also contributed by playing a number of games with a positive attitude and results that bolstered my enthusiasm. So, too, was Carol Krucoff a spirit-lifter, offering comments on an early version of the manuscript.

Then there are the many whose spiritual journey has influenced my own. I think particularly of friends such as Kathleen Donofrio, Tim Brown, Jane Thibault, Carol Segrave, Connie Goldman, Zalman Schachter-Shalomi, Ram Dass, and several others I've met through the Omega Institute. Each of these splendid people has a spirit that knows how to play. So, too, do numerous inmates I met teaching at the Maryland State Penitentiary and other prisons. These friends maintain the joy of life under the most dire conditions. I hope "games for the soul" can be of some use to them.

A special thanks also goes to fellow travelers I've met in many a Twelve Step room. Their insights, and this excellent program, have triggered ideas for certain games and enhanced my life immeasurably.

A potent trio has helped to midwife the book. Lynn Rosen is my valued agent, guide, and friend. Without her support and professional talents, this book might never have been. In Laurie Abkemeier, I could not be blessed with a more savvy and enthusiastic editor. Lisa M. Flaherty has been invaluable as a research associate, colleague, and trusted friend. She tested out these games with me, providing useful comments, and labored lovingly over those manuscript details that can drive an author crazy. All the while, her mother, Mary Theresa Flaherty, gave behind-the-scenes support and prayer.

A special thanks goes to my daughter, Sarah Chang-Ye Leder. You have been a source of never-ending delight. And what to say to her mother and my wife, Janice McLane? Your suggestions have informed the book. Your challenges have made it sharper. Your encouragement sustained me in its writing. Your love transforms my life.

234

About the Author

Drew Leder, M.D., Ph.D. is an associate professor of Western and Eastern philosophy at Loyola College in Maryland. He is the author or editor of numerous books, including *Spiritual Passages: Embracing Life's Sacred Journey*. Articles by or about Dr. Leder have appeared in the *Washington Post,* the *Chicago Tribune,* and the *Baltimore Sun,* and he has been featured on national television and radio shows. He lives in Baltimore with his wife, Janice, and daughter, Sarah.

235